40 Best Machine Code Routines for the 64

40 Best Machine Code Routines for the 64

Mark Greenshields

Contents

Preface

This book is not intended to teach you machine code on the CBM 64. It contains 40 machine code routines that can be used in your Basic or machine code programs to do things that are not implemented in the standard BASIC or operating system in your Commodore 64.

The book includes a listing of Supermon which is a public domain assembler/disassembler written by Jim Butterfield (thanks Jim). It can be used to enter the programs in this book if you do not possess an assembler. The listings are all given twice: once in an assembled listing from the PAL assembler from Proline Software (this, along with POWER, is the best machine code development package that I have seen), and once in a disassembled version suitable for entering with Supermon or similar.

I hope that you find the book useful and that the routines help to improve your programs.

Acknowledgments

I would like to thank my parents Jack and Sheila Greenshields, my sister Louise, Graeme Douglas, William Drummond, Mark Kelly and all my relations for their encouragement.

M.G.

I would like to dedicate this book to my grandparents, Roy and Gracie Reid.

Supermon

There follows a listing of Supermon which is a public domain assembler/disassembler/monitor. Thanks to Jim Butterfield for this program. The Basic program which follows is used to enter this assembler. You will need this assembler or a similar one to enter all the programs in this book.

Supermon is listed as a hex dump, which is a listing of hexadecimal numbers. This makes it easy to enter into a Basic loader program.

To enter Supermon, type in the following commands in direct mode (where < return > means press the return key), and then type in the Basic loader and save it.

    POKE 43,1 < return >
    POKE 44,32 < return >
    POKE8192,0 < return >
    NEW < return >

Now run the loader and you will see the prompt:

    .0800 ?

You will see that the first number corresponds with the first number in the Supermon listing. This is where you type the data. The first three lines that you would type are as follows. Type the program in without spaces.

    .0800 ? 001A086400992293
    .0808 ? 121D1D1D1D535550
    .0810 ? 45522036342D4D4F

Don't worry if you don't understand what you are typing in. Just type exactly what is printed and it will work. It is worth it as writing machine code using an assembler is far easier than doing it by hand. Once you have finished typing in the program you will be prompted with:

SAVE TO TAPE OR DISK ?

Press T if you are using cassette and have a blank cassette in the recorder. Press D if you are using disk and make sure that a formatted disk with at least 11 blocks free is in the drive.

If you pressed T you will be prompted with PRESS PLAY ON TAPE and if you pressed D the drive will start whirring. The program is now being saved to tape or disk. If an error occurs then typing RUN100 will allow you to save the program again. It can be loaded in the normal way.

LOAD"SUPERMON",1 OR LOAD"SUPERMON",8

Then run the program. Some writing will appear on the screen and a '.' prompt will appear.

To make spare copies of Supermon just load the program and save it as if it was Basic.

Supermon is given here as a relocatable loader: it can be located anywhere in RAM. To adjust where it is to be located in memory, find the starting address and add 2065 to it. Use the following formula to calculate the two numbers necessary:

LO = INT(number/256)
HI = ((number/256)-LO)*256

Now POKE 55 with the value of LO and POKE 56 with the value of HI and run Supermon.

To restart Supermon, type SYS starting address + 1. The normal value to start Supermon is SYS 38893.

Instructions for using Supermon

Supermon commands are all one-letter commands usually

followed by parameters.

The first command that we will look at is 'A'. This stands for ASSEMBLE and is the most frequently used command in any assembler. It will be used for entering almost all the programs in this book. The syntax for 'A' is as follows:

A (start address in hex) (mnemonic) (operand).

e.g. A 1000 LDA #$10

The address is the starting address in hex. The mnemonic is the assembly language command and the operand is the number associated with the command if there is one.

After you press return from the first line, if it is incorrect syntax, the computer will prompt you with an 'A' and the next address. Therefore you need only enter the starting address, the assembler does the rest. To leave the assembly press the return key.

Here is a simple example program which shows you how the assembler works.

```
.A 1000 LDA #$00
.A 1002 STA $D020
.A 1005 STA $D021
.A 1008 RTS
```

This program makes the screen and the border black. Type it in to see how to use the assembler. If you make an error the computer will print a question mark. If this happens use the normal screen editor and change the mistake and delete the question mark. Press return and if the next address is prompted then the line is now correct.

Now that you have typed this in, you may want to save the program. The command to do this is 'S'. The syntax is as follows:

S"name",device,start,end + 1

The total length of the name must not exceed 16 or a question

3

mark will be printed. The device is the device that the computer is to save to: 01 is tape and 08 is disk. The 0's before the number are essential for correct syntax. The start is the starting address in hex of the save. The end + 1 is the end address plus 1 that the computer is to save to. The reason that you must save up to the end + 1 is that the ROM routine used to save to memory saves up to but not including the end address specified. All the parameters must be separated by a comma.

The next command is the command to execute a program in machine code from the assembler. It is 'G' and has the syntax:

   G address to start at.

If you want to return control to the monitor when the program has been run then make the last command of the program a BRK command instead of an RTS.

The next command allows you to see a program in memory. It is 'D' and has the syntax:

   D start

e.g. D 1000

This command clears the screen and prints a page of commands. To see more press D and return.

The next command is the same as 'D' except that it prints a continuous listing without clearing the screen. The command is 'P' and it has the syntax:

   P start end

It is mainly used when you want a printer listing. To print a disassembly to the printer type the following in Basic:

   OPEN4,4 : CMD4 : SYS38893

(The SYS assumes that the monitor is at its default position in memory. If it isn't, use your address.)

The printer will print something and then you can type what you want. You can use 'P' or 'M' (coming up next). To disable the printer when it has finished type 'X' < return > (explained later) and type CLOSE4. < return >.

Often you will want a listing of memory in hex (which Supermon was listed in). This is done with the 'M' command which has the syntax:

M start end

where start and end are in hex. This command may also be used to the printer. You may also change memory by using this command and then typing over values and pressing return at the end of each line.

The monitor has a command to fill areas of memory with a number. It is 'F' and it has the syntax:

F start end byte

where start and end are addresses in hex and byte is a byte in hex.

Supermon can move parts of memory to another part. The command is 'T' which stands for transfer memory. It has the syntax:

T oldstart oldend newstart

where oldstart, oldend and newstart are addresses in hex.

If you want to find the contents of the registers at any time, type the command 'R' on its own.

If you are working in the assembler and you want to load a program into memory where it came from, there are two ways to do this:

1. return to Basic and type LOAD"name",device,1

e.g. To load the file hello from tape type LOAD"HELLO",1,1

2. use the command 'L' in the monitor. It has the syntax:

L"name",device

where device is 01 for tape and 08 for disk.

To exit the assembler and return to Basic type X <return> or press run/stop and restore.

Summary of SUPERMON commands.

Command Syntax	Meaning	
A	Assemble Mnemonics into memory	A 1000 LDA #$10
D	Disassemble memory	D 1000
M	Display hex from memory	M 1000 2000
S	Save memory to device	S"name",08,1000,2000
L	Load memory from device	L"name",01
P	Print disassembly of memory	P 1000 2000
F	Fill memory	F 3000 4000 FF
T	Transfer memory to memory	T 1000 2000 C000
X	Exit to Basic	X
R	Register display	R
G	Goto address	G FFD2

```
1 HE$="0123456789ABCDEF"
10 PRINT"(CLR)"
20 FORA=2049TO4587STEP8
30 GOSUB1000:REM CONVERT ADDRESS TO HEX
IN H$
40 PRINT".";H$;:INPUT A$:REM 8 HEX NUMBE
RS
50 FORX=1TO16STEP2
```

```
60 B$=MID$(A$,X,2)
70 GOSUB2000:REM CONVERT HEX NO. TO DECI
MAL
80 POKEA+X/2,HEX
90 NEXT:NEXT
100 INPUT"SAVE TO TAPE OR DISK";TD$
110 IFTD$="D"ORTD$="T"THEN120
115 GOTO100
120 IFTD$="D"THENDEV=8
130 IFTD$="T"THENDEV=1
140 FORA=0TO34:READB:POKEA+49152,B:NEXT:
POKE49153,DEV:INPUT"ARE YOU SURE";S$
150 IFS$="N"THEN100
160 SYS49152: REM SAVE ASSEMBLER
170 PRINT"MACHINE CODE SAVED"
180 PRINT"IT MAY BE LOADED FROM TAPE OR
DISK IN THE NORMAL WAY LIKE A BASIC"
190 PRINT"PROGRAM AND THEN RUN"
200 END
1000 N1=INT(A/4096):N6=(A/4096-N1)*16:N2
=INT(N6):N3=INT((N6-N2)*16)
1010 N4=(((N6-N2)*16)-N3)*16
1030 H$=MID$(HE$,N1+1,1)+MID$(HE$,N2+1,1
)+MID$(HE$,N3+1,1)+MID$(HE$,N4+1,1)
1040 RETURN
2000 FORV=1TO16:B=V-1:IFLEFT$(B$,1)=MID$
(HE$,V,1)THEN2020
2010 NEXT
2020 HEX=B*16
2030 FORV=1TO16:B=V-1:IFRIGHT$(B$,1)=MID
$(HE$,V,1)THEN2050
2040 NEXT
2050 HEX=HEX+B
2060 PRINT HEX
2070 RETURN
10000 DATA 162,1,160,1,32,186,255,162,26
,160,192,169,8,32,189,255,162,236,160
10010 DATA 17,169,251,32,216,255,96,83,8
5,80,69,82,77,79,78,0
20000 OPEN15,8,15:INPUT#15,A$,B$,C$,D$:P
RINTA$,B$,C$,D$:CLOSE15
```

```
B*
      PC   SR  AC  XR  YR  SP
.;97FE 33  ØØ  28  ØØ  F6
.

.:Ø8ØØ 00  1A  Ø8  64  ØØ  99  22  93
.:Ø8Ø8 12  1D  1D  1D  1D  53  55  5Ø
.:Ø81Ø 45  52  2Ø  36  34  2D  4D  4F
.:Ø818 4E  ØØ  31  Ø8  6E  ØØ  99  22
.:Ø82Ø 11  2Ø  2Ø  2Ø  2Ø  2Ø  2Ø  2Ø
.:Ø828 2Ø  2Ø  2Ø  2Ø  2Ø  2Ø  2Ø  2Ø
.:Ø83Ø ØØ  4B  Ø8  78  ØØ  99  22  11
.:Ø838 2Ø  2E  2E  4A  49  4D  2Ø  42
.:Ø84Ø 55  54  54  45  52  46  49  45
.:Ø848 4C  44  ØØ  66  Ø8  82  ØØ  9E
.:Ø85Ø 28  C2  28  34  33  29  AA  32
.:Ø858 35  36  AC  C2  28  34  34  29
.:Ø86Ø AA  31  32  37  29  ØØ  ØØ  ØØ
.:Ø868 AA  AA  AA  AA  AA  AA  AA  AA
.:Ø87Ø AA  AA  AA  AA  AA  AA  AA  AA
.:Ø878 AA  AA  AA  AA  AA  AA  AA  AA
.:Ø88Ø A5  2D  85  22  A5  2E  85  23
.:Ø888 A5  37  85  24  A5  38  85  25
.:Ø89Ø AØ  ØØ  A5  22  DØ  Ø2  C6  23
.:Ø898 C6  22  B1  22  DØ  3C  A5  22
.:Ø8AØ DØ  Ø2  C6  23  C6  22  B1  22
.:Ø8A8 FØ  21  85  26  A5  22  DØ  Ø2
.:Ø8BØ C6  23  C6  22  B1  22  18  65
.:Ø8B8 24  AA  A5  26  65  25  48  A5
.:Ø8CØ 37  DØ  Ø2  C6  38  C6  37  68
.:Ø8C8 91  37  8A  48  A5  37  DØ  Ø2
.:Ø8DØ C6  38  C6  37  68  91  37  18
.:Ø8D8 9Ø  B6  C9  4F  DØ  ED  A5  37
.:Ø8EØ 85  33  A5  38  85  34  6C  37
.:Ø8E8 ØØ  4F  4F  4F  4F  AD  E6  FF
.:Ø8FØ ØØ  8D  16  Ø3  AD  E7  FF  ØØ
.:Ø8F8 8D  17  Ø3  A9  8Ø  2Ø  9Ø  FF
.:Ø9ØØ ØØ  ØØ  D8  68  8D  3E  Ø2  68
.:Ø9Ø8 8D  3D  Ø2  68  8D  3C  Ø2  68
.:Ø91Ø 8D  3B  Ø2  68  AA  68  A8  38
```

```
.:0928 02 20 57 FD 00 A2 42 A9
.:0930 2A 20 57 FA 00 A9 52 D0
.:0938 34 E6 C1 D0 06 E6 C2 D0
.:0940 02 E6 26 60 20 CF FF C9
.:0948 0D D0 F8 68 68 EA EA EA
.:0950 EA EA A9 00 00 85 26 A2
.:0958 0D A9 2E 20 57 FA 00 EA
.:0960 EA EA EA EA 20 3E F8 00
.:0968 C9 2E F0 F9 C9 20 F0 F5
.:0970 A2 0E DD B7 FF 00 D0 0C
.:0978 8A 0A AA BD C7 FF 00 48
.:0980 BD C6 FF 00 48 60 CA 10
.:0988 EC 4C ED FA 00 A5 C1 8D
.:0990 3A 02 A5 C2 8D 39 02 60
.:0998 A9 08 85 1D A0 00 00 20
.:09A0 54 FD 00 B1 C1 20 48 FA
.:09A8 00 20 33 F8 00 C6 1D D0
.:09B0 F1 60 20 88 FA 00 90 0B
.:09B8 A2 00 00 81 C1 C1 C1 F0
.:09C0 03 4C ED FA 00 20 33 F8
.:09C8 00 C6 1D 60 A9 3B 85 C1
.:09D0 A9 02 85 C2 A9 05 60 98
.:09D8 48 20 57 FD 00 68 A2 2E
.:09E0 4C 57 FA 00 EA EA EA EA
.:09E8 EA A2 00 00 BD EA FF 00
.:09F0 20 D2 FF E8 E0 16 D0 F5
.:09F8 A0 3B 20 C2 F8 00 AD 39
.:0A00 02 20 48 FA 00 AD 3A 02
.:0A08 20 48 FA 00 20 B7 F8 00
.:0A10 20 8D F8 00 F0 5C 20 3E
.:0A18 F8 00 20 79 FA 00 90 33
.:0A20 20 69 FA 00 20 3E F8 00
.:0A28 20 79 FA 00 90 28 20 69
.:0A30 FA 00 EA EA EA EA EA 20
.:0A38 E1 FF F0 3C A6 26 D0 38
.:0A40 A5 C3 C5 C1 A5 C4 E5 C2
.:0A48 90 2E A0 3A 20 C2 F8 00
.:0A50 20 41 FA 00 20 8B F8 00
.:0A58 F0 E0 4C ED FA 00 20 79
.:0A60 FA 00 90 03 20 80 F8 00
.:0A68 20 B7 F8 00 D0 07 20 79
```

```
.:0A70 FA 00 90 EB A9 08 85 1D
.:0A78 20 3E F8 00 20 A1 F8 00
.:0A80 D0 F8 4C 47 F8 00 20 CF
.:0A88 FF C9 0D F0 0C C9 20 D0
.:0A90 D1 20 79 FA 00 90 03 20
.:0A98 80 F8 00 EA EA EA EA EA
.:0AA0 AE 3F 02 9A 78 AD 39 02
.:0AA8 48 AD 3A 02 48 AD 3B 02
.:0AB0 48 AD 3C 02 AE 3D 02 AC
.:0AB8 3E 02 40 EA EA EA EA EA
.:0AC0 AE 3F 02 9A 6C 02 A0 A0
.:0AC8 01 84 BA 84 B9 88 84 B7
.:0AD0 84 90 84 93 A9 40 85 BB
.:0AD8 A9 02 85 BC 20 CF FF C9
.:0AE0 20 F0 F9 C9 0D F0 38 C9
.:0AE8 22 D0 14 20 CF FF C9 22
.:0AF0 F0 10 C9 0D F0 29 91 BB
.:0AF8 E6 B7 C8 C0 10 D0 EC 4C
.:0B00 ED FA 00 20 CF FF C9 0D
.:0B08 F0 16 C9 2C D0 DC 20 88
.:0B10 FA 00 29 0F F0 E9 C9 03
.:0B18 F0 E5 85 BA 20 CF FF C9
.:0B20 0D 60 6C 30 03 6C 32 03
.:0B28 20 96 F9 00 D0 D4 EA EA
.:0B30 EA EA EA A9 00 00 20 EF
.:0B38 F9 00 A5 90 29 10 D0 C4
.:0B40 4C 47 F8 00 20 96 F9 00
.:0B48 C9 2C D0 BA 20 79 FA 00
.:0B50 20 69 FA 00 20 CF FF C9
.:0B58 2C D0 AD 20 79 FA 00 A5
.:0B60 C1 85 AE A5 C2 85 AF 20
.:0B68 69 FA 00 20 CF FF C9 0D
.:0B70 D0 98 EA EA EA EA EA 20
.:0B78 F2 F9 00 4C 47 F8 00 A5
.:0B80 C2 20 48 FA 00 A5 C1 48
.:0B88 4A 4A 4A 4A 20 60 FA 00
.:0B90 AA 68 29 0F 20 60 FA 00
.:0B98 48 8A 20 D2 FF 68 4C D2
.:0BA0 FF 09 30 C9 3A 90 02 69
.:0BA8 06 60 A2 02 B5 C0 48 B5
.:0BB0 C2 95 C0 68 95 C2 CA D0
```

```
.:0BB8 F3 60 20 88 FA 00 90 02
.:0BC0 85 C2 20 88 FA 00 90 02
.:0BC8 85 C1 60 A9 00 00 85 2A
.:0BD0 20 3E F8 00 C9 20 D0 09
.:0BD8 20 3E F8 00 C9 20 D0 0E
.:0BE0 18 60 20 AF FA 00 0A 0A
.:0BE8 0A 0A 85 2A 20 3E F8 00
.:0BF0 20 AF FA 00 05 2A 38 60
.:0BF8 C9 3A 90 02 69 08 29 0F
.:0C00 60 A2 02 2C A2 00 00 B4
.:0C08 C1 D0 08 B4 C2 D0 02 E6
.:0C10 26 D6 C2 D6 C1 60 20 3E
.:0C18 F8 00 C9 20 F0 F9 60 A9
.:0C20 00 00 8D 00 00 01 20 CC
.:0C28 FA 00 20 8F FA 00 20 7C
.:0C30 FA 00 90 09 60 20 3E F8
.:0C38 00 20 79 FA 00 B0 DE AE
.:0C40 3F 02 9A EA EA EA EA EA
.:0C48 A9 3F 20 D2 FF 4C 47 F8
.:0C50 00 20 54 FD 00 CA D0 FA
.:0C58 60 E6 C3 D0 02 E6 C4 60
.:0C60 A2 02 B5 C0 48 B5 27 95
.:0C68 C0 68 95 27 CA D0 F3 60
.:0C70 A5 C3 A4 C4 38 E9 02 B0
.:0C78 0E 88 90 0B A5 28 A4 29
.:0C80 4C 33 FB 00 A5 C3 A4 C4
.:0C88 38 E5 C1 85 1E 98 E5 C2
.:0C90 A8 05 1E 60 20 D4 FA 00
.:0C98 20 69 FA 00 20 E5 FA 00
.:0CA0 20 0C FB 00 20 E5 FA 00
.:0CA8 20 2F FB 00 20 69 FA 00
.:0CB0 90 15 A6 26 D0 64 20 28
.:0CB8 FB 00 90 5F A1 C1 81 C3
.:0CC0 20 05 FB 00 20 33 F8 00
.:0CC8 D0 EB 20 28 FB 00 18 A5
.:0CD0 1E 65 C3 85 C3 98 65 C4
.:0CD8 85 C4 20 0C FB 00 A6 26
.:0CE0 D0 3D A1 C1 81 C3 20 28
.:0CE8 FB 00 B0 34 20 B8 FA 00
.:0CF0 20 BB FA 00 4C 7D FB 00
.:0CF8 20 D4 FA 00 20 69 FA 00
```

```
.:0D00 20 E5 FA 00 20 69 FA 00
.:0D08 20 3E F8 00 20 88 FA 00
.:0D10 90 14 85 1D A6 26 D0 11
.:0D18 20 2F FB 00 90 0C A5 1D
.:0D20 81 C1 20 33 F8 00 D0 EE
.:0D28 4C ED FA 00 4C 47 F8 00
.:0D30 20 D4 FA 00 20 69 FA 00
.:0D38 20 E5 FA 00 20 69 FA 00
.:0D40 20 3E F8 00 A2 00 00 20
.:0D48 3E F8 00 C9 27 D0 14 20
.:0D50 3E F8 00 9D 10 02 E8 20
.:0D58 CF FF C9 0D F0 22 E0 20
.:0D60 D0 F1 F0 1C 8E 00 00 01
.:0D68 20 8F FA 00 90 C6 9D 10
.:0D70 02 E8 20 CF FF C9 0D F0
.:0D78 09 20 88 FA 00 90 B6 E0
.:0D80 20 D0 EC 86 1C EA EA EA
.:0D88 EA EA 20 57 FD 00 A2 00
.:0D90 00 A0 00 00 B1 C1 DD 10
.:0D98 02 D0 0C C8 E8 E4 1C D0
.:0DA0 F3 20 41 FA 00 20 54 FD
.:0DA8 00 20 33 F8 00 A6 26 D0
.:0DB0 8D 20 2F FB 00 B0 DD 4C
.:0DB8 47 F8 00 20 D4 FA 00 85
.:0DC0 20 A5 C2 85 21 A2 00 00
.:0DC8 86 28 A9 93 20 D2 FF EA
.:0DD0 EA EA EA EA A9 16 85 1D
.:0DD8 20 6A FC 00 20 CA FC 00
.:0DE0 85 C1 84 C2 C6 1D D0 F2
.:0DE8 A9 91 20 D2 FF 4C 47 F8
.:0DF0 00 A0 2C 20 C2 F8 00 20
.:0DF8 54 FD 00 20 41 FA 00 20
.:0E00 54 FD 00 A2 00 00 A1 C1
.:0E08 20 D9 FC 00 48 20 1F FD
.:0E10 00 68 20 35 FD 00 A2 06
.:0E18 E0 03 D0 12 A4 1F F0 0E
.:0E20 A5 2A C9 E8 B1 C1 B0 1C
.:0E28 20 C2 FC 00 88 D0 F2 06
.:0E30 2A 90 0E BD 2A FF 00 20
.:0E38 A5 FD 00 BD 30 FF 00 F0
.:0E40 03 20 A5 FD 00 CA D0 D5
```

```
.:ØE48 6Ø 2Ø CD FC ØØ AA E8 DØ
.:ØE5Ø Ø1 C8 98 2Ø C2 FC ØØ 8A
.:ØE58 86 1C 2Ø 48 FA ØØ A6 1C
.:ØE6Ø 6Ø A5 1F 38 A4 C2 AA 1Ø
.:ØE68 Ø1 88 65 C1 9Ø Ø1 C8 6Ø
.:ØE7Ø A8 4A 9Ø ØB 4A BØ 17 C9
.:ØE78 22 FØ 13 29 Ø7 Ø9 8Ø 4A
.:ØE8Ø AA BD D9 FE ØØ BØ Ø4 4A
.:ØE88 4A 4A 4A 29 ØF DØ Ø4 AØ
.:ØE9Ø 8Ø A9 ØØ ØØ AA BD 1D FF
.:ØE98 ØØ 85 2A 29 Ø3 85 1F 98
.:ØEAØ 29 8F AA 98 AØ Ø3 EØ 8A
.:ØEA8 FØ ØB 4A 9Ø Ø8 4A 4A Ø9
.:ØEBØ 2Ø 88 DØ FA C8 88 DØ F2
.:ØEB8 6Ø B1 C1 2Ø C2 FC ØØ A2
.:ØECØ Ø1 2Ø FE FA ØØ C4 1F C8
.:ØEC8 9Ø F1 A2 Ø3 CØ Ø4 9Ø F2
.:ØEDØ 6Ø A8 B9 37 FF ØØ 85 28
.:ØED8 B9 77 FF ØØ 85 29 A9 ØØ
.:ØEEØ ØØ AØ Ø5 Ø6 29 26 28 2A
.:ØEE8 88 DØ F8 69 3F 2Ø D2 FF
.:ØEFØ CA DØ EC A9 2Ø 2C A9 ØD
.:ØEF8 4C D2 FF 2Ø D4 FA ØØ 2Ø
.:ØFØØ 69 FA ØØ 2Ø E5 FA ØØ 2Ø
.:ØFØ8 69 FA ØØ A2 ØØ ØØ 86 28
.:ØF1Ø EA EA EA EA EA 2Ø 57 FD
.:ØF18 ØØ 2Ø 72 FC ØØ 2Ø CA FC
.:ØF2Ø ØØ 85 C1 84 C2 2Ø E1 FF
.:ØF28 FØ Ø5 2Ø 2F FB ØØ BØ E9
.:ØF3Ø 4C 47 F8 ØØ 2Ø D4 FA ØØ
.:ØF38 A9 Ø3 85 1D 2Ø 3E F8 ØØ
.:ØF4Ø 2Ø A1 F8 ØØ DØ F8 A5 2Ø
.:ØF48 85 C1 A5 21 85 C2 4C 46
.:ØF5Ø FC ØØ C5 28 FØ Ø3 2Ø D2
.:ØF58 FF 6Ø 2Ø D4 FA ØØ 2Ø 69
.:ØF6Ø FA ØØ 8E 11 Ø2 A2 Ø3 2Ø
.:ØF68 CC FA ØØ 48 CA DØ F9 A2
.:ØF7Ø Ø3 68 38 E9 3F AØ Ø5 4A
.:ØF78 6E 11 Ø2 6E 1Ø Ø2 88 DØ
.:ØF8Ø F6 CA DØ ED A2 Ø2 2Ø CF
.:ØF88 FF C9 ØD FØ 1E C9 2Ø FØ
```

```
.:ØF90 F5 20 DØ FE ØØ BØ ØF 20
.:ØF98 9C FA ØØ A4 C1 84 C2 85
.:ØFAØ C1 A9 30 9D 10 Ø2 E8 9D
.:ØFA8 10 Ø2 E8 DØ DB 86 28 A2
.:ØFBØ ØØ ØØ 86 26 FØ Ø4 E6 26
.:ØFB8 FØ 75 A2 ØØ ØØ 86 1D A5
.:ØFCØ 26 20 D9 FC ØØ A6 2A 86
.:ØFC8 29 AA BC 37 FF ØØ BD 77
.:ØFDØ FF ØØ 20 B9 FE ØØ DØ E3
.:ØFD8 A2 Ø6 EØ Ø3 DØ 19 A4 1F
.:ØFEØ FØ 15 A5 2A C9 E8 A9 30
.:ØFE8 BØ 21 20 BF FE ØØ DØ CC
.:ØFFØ 20 C1 FE ØØ DØ C7 88 DØ
.:ØFF8 EB Ø6 2A 9Ø ØB BC 30 FF
.:1ØØØ ØØ BD 2A FF ØØ 20 B9 FE
.:1ØØ8 ØØ DØ B5 CA DØ D1 FØ ØA
.:1Ø1Ø 20 B8 FE ØØ DØ AB 20 B8
.:1Ø18 FE ØØ DØ A6 A5 28 C5 1D
.:1Ø2Ø DØ AØ 20 69 FA ØØ A4 1F
.:1Ø28 FØ 28 A5 29 C9 9D DØ 1A
.:1Ø3Ø 20 1C FB ØØ 9Ø ØA 98 DØ
.:1Ø38 Ø4 A5 1E 10 ØA 4C ED FA
.:1Ø4Ø ØØ C8 DØ FA A5 1E 10 F6
.:1Ø48 A4 1F DØ Ø3 B9 C2 ØØ ØØ
.:1Ø5Ø 91 C1 88 DØ F8 A5 26 91
.:1Ø58 C1 20 CA FC ØØ 85 C1 84
.:1Ø6Ø C2 EA EA EA EA EA AØ 41
.:1Ø68 20 C2 F8 ØØ 20 54 FD ØØ
.:1Ø7Ø 20 41 FA ØØ 20 54 FD ØØ
.:1Ø78 EA EA EA EA EA 4C BØ FD
.:1Ø8Ø ØØ A8 20 BF FE ØØ DØ 11
.:1Ø88 98 FØ ØE 86 1C A6 1D DD
.:1Ø9Ø 10 Ø2 Ø8 E8 86 1D A6 1C
.:1Ø98 28 60 C9 3Ø 9Ø Ø3 C9 47
.:1ØAØ 60 38 60 4Ø Ø2 45 Ø3 DØ
.:1ØA8 Ø8 4Ø Ø9 3Ø 22 45 33 DØ
.:1ØBØ Ø8 4Ø Ø9 4Ø Ø2 45 33 DØ
.:1ØB8 Ø8 4Ø Ø9 4Ø Ø2 45 B3 DØ
.:1ØCØ Ø8 4Ø Ø9 ØØ ØØ 22 44 33
.:1ØC8 DØ 8C 44 ØØ ØØ 11 22 44
.:1ØDØ 33 DØ 8C 44 9A 10 22 44
```

14

```
.:10D8 33 D0 08 40 09 10 22 44
.:10E0 33 D0 08 40 09 62 13 78
.:10E8 A9 00 00 21 81 82 00 00
.:10F0 00 00 59 4D 91 92 86 4A
.:10F8 85 9D 2C 29 2C 23 28 24
.:1100 59 00 00 58 24 24 00 00
.:1108 1C 8A 1C 23 5D 8B 1B A1
.:1110 9D 8A 1D 23 9D 8B 1D A1
.:1118 00 00 29 19 AE 69 A8 19
.:1120 23 24 53 1B 23 24 53 19
.:1128 A1 00 00 1A 5B 5B A5 69
.:1130 24 24 AE AE A8 AD 29 00
.:1138 00 7C 00 00 15 9C 6D 9C
.:1140 A5 69 29 53 84 13 34 11
.:1148 A5 69 23 A0 D8 62 5A 48
.:1150 26 62 94 88 54 44 C8 54
.:1158 68 44 E8 94 00 00 B4 08
.:1160 84 74 B4 28 6E 74 F4 CC
.:1168 4A 72 F2 A4 8A 00 00 AA
.:1170 A2 A2 74 74 74 72 44 68
.:1178 B2 32 B2 00 00 22 00 00
.:1180 1A 1A 26 26 72 72 88 C8
.:1188 C4 CA 26 48 44 44 A2 C8
.:1190 3A 3B 52 4D 47 58 4C 53
.:1198 54 46 48 44 50 2C 41 42
.:11A0 F9 00 35 F9 00 CC F8 00
.:11A8 F7 F8 00 56 F9 00 89 F9
.:11B0 00 F4 F9 00 0C FA 00 3E
.:11B8 FB 00 92 FB 00 C0 FB 00
.:11C0 38 FC 00 5B FD 00 8A FD
.:11C8 00 AC FD 00 46 F8 00 FF
.:11D0 F7 00 ED F7 00 0D 20 20
.:11D8 20 50 43 20 20 53 52 20
.:11E0 41 43 20 58 52 20 59 52
.:11E8 20 53 50 45 52 22 20 20
```

ROM Routines

The routines in this book use various ROM routines to function. They are as follows:

$AEFD: Check if the next character is a comma and skip it. Otherwise print SYNTAX ERROR and return to Basic.

$AD8A: Read next expression (variable, number, etc.) into the FAC.

$B7F7: Change the value in the FAC into a 16 bit integer (0-65535). If the number is too big then print illegal quantity error and return to Basic. Otherwise put the low byte of the number into $14 and the high byte into $15.

$B79E: Read the next expression in the BASIC text and put it as a 8 bit integer in the X register. If the number is greater than 255 then print Illegal quantity error and return to Basic.

$B7EB: This routine reads two expressions or numbers separated by a comma from the Basic text. The first is a 16 bit number and the second is an 8 bit number. The 16 bit number is stored in $14 and $15 and the 8 bit number is stored in the X register. If either or both of the numbers are out of their ranges then the program will stop and print an illegal quantity error. If the comma is missing a syntax error with be displayed. Both these errors return control to Basic.

$E1D4: This routine gets the file name, the device number and the secondary address from the Basic text. It gives an error if any of the above are wrong. It is used in preparation for loading, saving or verifying a program, as in MSAVE/MLOAD/MVERIFY.

1. Fill

The following routine allows you to fill an area of memory with a byte. It is called by the following command:

SYS 28672,start address, end address, byte

e.g. to fill the text screen with 'A' characters and the colour screen with 1 (white), type the following:

SYS 28672,1024,2023,1
SYS 28672,55296,56295,1

An error will be given if any of the numbers are too big or negative.

```
PAL (C)1979 BRAD TEMPLETON
2
20:     7000                        .OPT P,OO
30:     7000                        *=      $7000
                            ;FILL ROUTINE
                            ;
                            ;USES $FB AND $FC
                            ;STORE TOP ADDRESS IN
                            ;828 AND 829
90:     7000 20 FD AE               JSR     $AEFD
                            ;SCAN PAST COMMA
110:    7003 20 8A AD               JSR     $AD8A
                            ;READ NUMBER AND PUT
                            ;INTO FAC
140:    7006 20 F7 B7               JSR     $B7F7
                            ;GET NUMBER FROM FAC
                            ; AND PUT IN $14 AND $15
170:    7009 A5 14                  LDA     $14
170:    700B 85 FB                  STA     $FB
```

```
180:    700D A5 15              LDA   $15
180:    700F 85 FC              STA   $FC
                            ;
200:    7011 20 FD AE           JSR   $AEFD
                            ;SCAN PAST COMMA
220:    7014 20 8A AD           JSR   $AD8A
230:    7017 20 F7 B7           JSR   $B7F7
240:    701A A5 14              LDA   $14
240:    701C 8D 3C 03           STA   828
250:    701F A5 15              LDA   $15
250:    7021 8D 3D 03           STA   829
                            ;
270:    7024 20 FD AE           JSR   $AEFD
280:    7027 20 8A AD           JSR   $AD8A
290:    702A 20 F7 B7           JSR   $B7F7
300:    702D A5 15              LDA   $15
300:    702F F0 03              BEQ   MORE
300:    7031 4C 48 B2           JMP   $B248
                            ;$B248 IS IQANT ERROR
320:    7034 A5 14      MORE     LDA   $14
320:    7036 8D 3E 03            STA   830
330:    7039 A0 00      LOOP     LDY   #0
340:    703B AD 3E 03            LDA   830
350:    703E 91 FB               STA   ($FB),Y
360:    7040 20 57 70           JSR   ADD
370:    7043 A5 FB               LDA   $FB
370:    7045 CD 3C 03           CMP   828
370:    7048 F0 03              BEQ   CHECK
380:    704A 4C 39 70           JMP   LOOP
390:    704D A5 FC      CHECK    LDA   $FC
390:    704F CD 3D 03           CMP   829
390:    7052 F0 0B              BEQ   FINISH
400:    7054 4C 39 70           JMP   LOOP
410:    7057 E6 FB      ADD      INC   $FB
410:    7059 F0 01              BEQ   FCPLUS1
420:    705B 60                 RTS
430:    705C E6 FC      FCPLUS1  INC   $FC
430:    705E 60                 RTS
440:    705F 60         FINISH   RTS
]7000-7060
```

```
B*
    PC  SR AC XR YR SP
.;97FE 72 00 00 01 F6

.
7000 20 FD AE       JSR $AEFD
7003 20 8A AD       JSR $AD8A
7006 20 F7 B7       JSR $B7F7
7009 A5 14          LDA $14
700B 85 FB          STA $FB
700D A5 15          LDA $15
700F 85 FC          STA $FC
7011 20 FD AE       JSR $AEFD
7014 20 8A AD       JSR $AD8A
7017 20 F7 B7       JSR $B7F7
701A A5 14          LDA $14
701C 8D 3C 03       STA $033C
701F A5 15          LDA $15
7021 8D 3D 03       STA $033D
7024 20 FD AE       JSR $AEFD
7027 20 8A AD       JSR $AD8A
702A 20 F7 B7       JSR $B7F7
702D A5 15          LDA $15
702F F0 03          BEQ $7034
7031 4C 48 B2       JMP $B248
7034 A5 14          LDA $14
7036 8D 3E 03       STA $033E
7039 A0 00          LDY #$00
703B AD 3E 03       LDA $033E
703E 91 FB          STA ($FB),Y
7040 20 57 70       JSR $7057
7043 A5 FB          LDA $FB
7045 CD 3C 03       CMP $033C
7048 F0 03          BEQ $704D
704A 4C 39 70       JMP $7039
704D A5 FC          LDA $FC
704F CD 3D 03       CMP $033D
7052 F0 0B          BEQ $705F
7054 4C 39 70       JMP $7039
7057 E6 FB          INC $FB
7059 F0 01          BEQ $705C
```

19

2. Move

The following routine allows you to move an area of memory to another location. It has the syntax:

SYS 24576,start,finish,destination address.

e.g. to move the contents of the screen to 16384 type the following:

SYS 24576,1024,2023,16384

The three numbers or variables must be no bigger than 65535. If they are bigger then an error will be printed and control will return to Basic.

```
PAL (C)1979 BRAD TEMPLETON
2
20:     6000                        .OPT P,00
30:     6000                        *=   $6000
                                 I
                                 IROUTINE TO MOVE ONE
                                 I AREA OF
                                 IMEMORY TO ANOTHER
                                 I
                                 ISCAN COMMA
90:     6000 20 FD AE             JSR   $AEFD
100:    6003 20 8A AD             JSR   $AD8A
110:    6006 20 F7 B7             JSR   $B7F7
120:    6009 A5 14                LDA   $14
130:    600B 8D 78 60             STA   TEMP
140:    600E A5 15                LDA   $15
150:    6010 8D 79 60             STA   TEMP+1
                                 I
165:    6013 20 FD AE             JSR   $AEFD
```

```
170:    6016 20 8A AD              JSR   *AD8A
180:    6019 20 F7 B7              JSR   *B7F7
190:    601C A5 14                 LDA   *14
200:    601E 8D 7A 60              STA   TEMP+2
210:    6021 A5 15                 LDA   *15
220:    6023 8D 7B 60              STA   TEMP+3
225:    6026 20 FD AE              JSR   *AEFD
230:    6029 20 8A AD              JSR   *AD8A
240:    602C 20 F7 B7              JSR   *B7F7
250:    602F A5 14                 LDA   *14
260:    6031 8D 7C 60              STA   TEMP+4
270:    6034 A5 15                 LDA   *15
280:    6036 8D 7D 60              STA   TEMP+5
                                   ;
291:    6039 AD 78 60              LDA   TEMP
291:    603C 85 FB                 STA   *FB
292:    603E AD 79 60              LDA   TEMP+1
292:    6041 85 FC                 STA   *FC
293:    6043 AD 7C 60              LDA   TEMP+4
293:    6046 85 FD                 STA   *FD
294:    6048 AD 7D 60              LDA   TEMP+5
294:    604B 85 FE                 STA   *FE
300:    604D A0 00                 LDY   #0
310:    604F B1 FB          LOOP   LDA   (*FB),Y
320:    6051 91 FD                 STA   (*FD),Y
330:    6053 20 60 60              JSR   ADDONE
340:    6056 A5 FB                 LDA   *FB
350:    6058 CD 7A 60              CMP   TEMP+2
360:    605B F0 10                 BEQ   CHECK
370:    605D 4C 4F 60              JMP   LOOP
                                   ;
                                   ;
400:    6060 E6 FB          ADDONE INC   *FB
410:    6062 D0 02                 BNE   MORE
420:    6064 E6 FC                 INC   *FC
430:    6066 E6 FD          MORE   INC   *FD
440:    6068 D0 02                 BNE   RETURN
450:    606A E6 FE                 INC   *FE
460:    606C 60            RETURN  RTS
                                   ;
                                   ;
```

```
490:    606D A5 FC      CHECK   LDA  #FC
500:    606F CD 7B 60           CMP  TEMP+3
510:    6072 F0 03              BEQ  FIN
520:    6074 4C 4F 60           JMP  LOOP
                        ;
                        ;
550:    6077            FIN     =    *
555:    6077 60                 RTS
560:    6078            TEMP    =    *
]6000-6078
```

READY.

```
B*
    PC   SR AC XR YR SP
.;97FE 72 00 00 01 F6
.
6000 20 FD AE      JSR  #AEFD
6003 20 8A AD      JSR  #AD8A
6006 20 F7 B7      JSR  #B7F7
6009 A5 14         LDA  #14
600B 8D 78 60      STA  #6078
600E A5 15         LDA  #15
6010 8D 79 60      STA  #6079
6013 20 FD AE      JSR  #AEFD
6016 20 8A AD      JSR  #AD8A
6019 20 F7 B7      JSR  #B7F7
601C A5 14         LDA  #14
601E 8D 7A 60      STA  #607A
6021 A5 15         LDA  #15
6023 8D 7B 60      STA  #607B
6026 20 FD AE      JSR  #AEFD
6029 20 8A AD      JSR  #AD8A
602C 20 F7 B7      JSR  #B7F7
602F A5 14         LDA  #14
6031 8D 7C 60      STA  #607C
6034 A5 15         LDA  #15
6036 8D 7D 60      STA  #607D
```

```
6039 AD 78 60    LDA $6078
603C 85 FB       STA $FB
603E AD 79 60    LDA $6079
6041 85 FC       STA $FC
6043 AD 7C 60    LDA $607C
6046 85 FD       STA $FD
6048 AD 7D 60    LDA $607D
604B 85 FE       STA $FE
604D A0 00       LDY #$00
604F B1 FB       LDA ($FB),Y
6051 91 FD       STA ($FD),Y
6053 20 60 60    JSR $6060
6056 A5 FB       LDA $FB
6058 CD 7A 60    CMP $607A
605B F0 10       BEQ $606D
605D 4C 4F 60    JMP $604F
6060 E6 FB       INC $FB
6062 D0 02       BNE $6066
6064 E6 FC       INC $FC
6066 E6 FD       INC $FD
6068 D0 02       BNE $606C
606A E6 FE       INC $FE
606C 60          RTS
606D A5 FC       LDA $FC
606F CD 7B 60    CMP $607B
6072 F0 03       BEQ $6077
6074 4C 4F 60    JMP $604F
6077 60          RTS
```

3. Pause

The following routine allows a listing to be stopped at any time. It will in fact stop any output to the screen that is printed. It works by interrupting the character out routine and check to see if the shift key has been pressed. If it has then it loops until the key has been released.

The syntax is SYS 960. To disable it press run/stop and restore simultaneously.

```
PAL (C)1979 BRAD TEMPLETON
2
20:     03C0                        .OPT P,00
30:     03C0                        *=    960
                            !
50:     03C0 A9 CB                  LDA   #<MAIN
60:     03C2 8D 26 03               STA   806
70:     03C5 A9 03                  LDA   #>MAIN
80:     03C7 8D 27 03               STA   807
90:     03CA 60                     RTS
                            !
110:    03CB 48          MAIN       PHA
110:    03CC 8A                     TXA
110:    03CD 48                     PHA
110:    03CE 98                     TYA
110:    03CF 48                     PHA
120:    03D0 AD 8D 02 LOOP          LDA   653
130:    03D3 C9 01                  CMP   #1
140:    03D5 F0 F9                  BEQ   LOOP
160:    03D7 68                     PLA
160:    03D8 A8                     TAY
160:    03D9 68                     PLA
160:    03DA AA                     TAX
```

```
160:     03DB 68                          PLA
170:     03DC 4C CA F1                    JMP   $F1CA
]03C0-03DF
```

READY.

```
B*
     PC  SR AC XR YR SP
.}97FE 72 00 00 01 F6
.
03C0 A9 CB              LDA #$CB
03C2 8D 26 03           STA $0326
03C5 A9 03              LDA #$03
03C7 8D 27 03           STA $0327
03CA 60                 RTS
03CB 48                 PHA
03CC 8A                 TXA
03CD 48                 PHA
03CE 98                 TYA
03CF 48                 PHA
03D0 AD 8D 02           LDA $028D
03D3 C9 01              CMP #$01
03D5 F0 F9              BEQ $03D0
03D7 68                 PLA
03D8 A8                 TAY
03D9 68                 PLA
03DA AA                 TAX
03DB 68                 PLA
03DC 4C CA F1           JMP $F1CA
```

4. Function keys

The following program allows you to put commands onto the function keys. It uses the IRQ interrupt to scan the keyboard. There are listings in PAL and Supermon format to see how the program works, but it is best to enter the program as the Basic loader which follows. Any of the three ways works equally well but it is easier to change the text to go on the function keys from the Basic listing.

To turn the keys on type SYS 49152 (for the Basic listing , SYS 24576 for the other two). To turn them off press run/stop and restore.

```
PAL (C)1979 BRAD TEMPLETON
2
20:    6000                      .OPT P,00
30:    6000                      *=   $6000
                         ;
                         ;ROUTINE TO SETUP
                         ;FUNCTION KEYS
                         ;
80:    6000 78                   SEI
90:    6001 A9 0D                LDA  #<MAIN
100:   6003 8D 14 03             STA  788
110:   6006 A9 60                LDA  #>MAIN
120:   6008 8D 15 03             STA  789
130:   600B 58                   CLI
140:   600C 60                   RTS
                         ;
                         ;
170:   600D 48          MAIN     PHA
180:   600E 8A                   TXA
190:   600F 48                   PHA
```

```
200:     6010 98              TYA
210:     6011 48              PHA
220:     6012 A5 C5           LDA   $C5
230:     6014 C5 FB           CMP   $FB
240:     6016 F0 52           BEQ   LOOP
250:     6018 85 FB           STA   $FB
260:     601A C9 03           CMP   #3
270:     601C D0 08           BNE   LOOP1
                       ;
290:     601E A9 30           LDA   #$30
300:     6020 8D 72 60        STA   C100
310:     6023 4C 47 60        JMP   PRINT
                       ;
330:     6026 C9 04    LOOP1  CMP   #4
340:     6028 D0 08           BNE   LOOP2
350:     602A A9 00           LDA   #0
360:     602C 8D 72 60        STA   C100
370:     602F 4C 47 60        JMP   PRINT
                       ;
390:     6032 C9 05    LOOP2  CMP   #5
400:     6034 D0 08           BNE   LOOP3
                       ;
420:     6036 A9 10           LDA   #$10
430:     6038 8D 72 60        STA   C100
440:     603B 4C 47 60        JMP   PRINT
                       ;
460:     603E C9 06    LOOP3  CMP   #6
470:     6040 D0 28           BNE   LOOP
480:     6042 A9 20           LDA   #$20
490:     6044 8D 72 60        STA   C100
                       ;
510:     6047 AD 8D 02 PRINT  LDA   $028D
520:     604A C9 01           CMP   #1
530:     604C D0 09           BNE   PUTON
                       ;
550:     604E AD 72 60        LDA   C100
560:     6051 18              CLC
560:     6052 69 08           ADC   #8
570:     6054 8D 72 60        STA   C100
                       ;
590:     6057 A2 00    PUTON  LDX   #0
```

27

```
600:      6059 AC 72 60             LDY   C100
610:      605C B9 73 60  LOP        LDA   C101,Y
620:      605F 9D 77 02             STA   $0277,X
630:      6062 E8                   INX
640:      6063 C8                   INY
650:      6064 E0 08                CPX   #$08
660:      6066 D0 F4                BNE   LOP
670:      6068 86 C6                STX   $C6
680:      606A 68         LOOP      PLA
690:      606B A8                   TAY
700:      606C 68                   PLA
710:      606D AA                   TAX
720:      606E 68                   PLA
730:      606F 4C 31 EA             JMP   $EA31
                              I
750:      6072 00         C100      .BYT  0
760:      6073 4C 49 53  C101       .ASC  "LIST"
760:      6077 0D 04 04             .BYT  13,4,4,4
770:      607B 52 55 4E             .ASC  "RUN"
770:      607E 0D 04 04             .BYT  13,4,4,4,4
780:      6083 50 52 49             .ASC  "PRINT"
780:      6088 04 04 04             .BYT  4,4,4
790:      608B 54 48 45             .ASC  "THEN"
790:      608F 04 04 04             .BYT  4,4,4,4
800:      6093 4C 4F 41             .ASC  "LOAD"
800:      6097 04 04 04             .BYT  4,4,4,4
810:      609B 53 41 56             .ASC  "SAVE"
810:      609F 04 04 04             .BYT  4,4,4,4
820:      60A3 56 45 52             .ASC  "VERIFY"
820:      60A9 04 04                .BYT  4,4
830:      60AB 47 4F 54             .ASC  "GOTO"
830:      60AF 04 04 04             .BYT  4,4,4,4
]6000-60B3
```

READY.

```
B*
   PC  SR AC XR YR SP
.¦97FE 72 00 00 01 F6
.
6000 78              SEI
6001 A9 0D           LDA #$0D
6003 8D 14 03        STA $0314
6006 A9 60           LDA #$60
6008 8D 15 03        STA $0315
600B 58              CLI
600C 60              RTS
600D 48              PHA
600E 8A              TXA
600F 48              PHA
6010 98              TYA
6011 48              PHA
6012 A5 C5           LDA $C5
6014 C5 FB           CMP $FB
6016 F0 52           BEQ $606A
6018 85 FB           STA $FB
601A C9 03           CMP #$03
601C D0 08           BNE $6026
601E A9 30           LDA #$30
6020 8D 72 60        STA $6072
6023 4C 47 60        JMP $6047
6026 C9 04           CMP #$04
6028 D0 08           BNE $6032
602A A9 00           LDA #$00
602C 8D 72 60        STA $6072
602F 4C 47 60        JMP $6047
6032 C9 05           CMP #$05
6034 D0 08           BNE $603E
6036 A9 10           LDA #$10
6038 8D 72 60        STA $6072
603B 4C 47 60        JMP $6047
603E C9 06           CMP #$06
6040 D0 28           BNE $606A
6042 A9 20           LDA #$20
6044 8D 72 60        STA $6072
6047 AD 8D 02        LDA $028D
604A C9 01           CMP #$01
```

```
604C DØ Ø9        BNE $6057
6Ø4E AD 72 6Ø     LDA $6072
6Ø51 18           CLC
6Ø52 69 Ø8        ADC #$Ø8
6Ø54 8D 72 6Ø     STA $6072
6Ø57 A2 ØØ        LDX #$ØØ
6Ø59 AC 72 6Ø     LDY $6072
6Ø5C B9 73 6Ø     LDA $6073,Y
6Ø5F 9D 77 Ø2     STA $Ø277,X
6Ø62 E8           INX
6Ø63 C8           INY
6Ø64 EØ Ø8        CPX #$Ø8
6Ø66 DØ F4        BNE $6Ø5C
6Ø68 86 C6        STX $C6
6Ø6A 68           PLA
6Ø6B A8           TAY
6Ø6C 68           PLA
6Ø6D AA           TAX
6Ø6E 68           PLA
6Ø6F 4C 31 EA     JMP $EA31
    .
    .
    .
    .
.:6072 ØØ 4C 49 53 54 ØD Ø4 Ø4
.:6Ø7A Ø4 52 55 4E ØD Ø4 Ø4 Ø4
.:6Ø82 Ø4 5Ø 52 49 4E 54 Ø4 Ø4
.:6Ø8A Ø4 54 48 45 4E Ø4 Ø4 Ø4
.:6Ø92 Ø4 4C 4F 41 44 Ø4 Ø4 Ø4
.:6Ø9A Ø4 53 41 56 45 Ø4 Ø4 Ø4
.:6ØA2 Ø4 56 45 52 49 46 59 Ø4
.:6ØAA Ø4 47 4F 54 4F Ø4 Ø4 Ø4
.:6ØB2 Ø4 ØØ ØØ ØØ ØØ ØØ FF ØØ
    .
```

30

```
10 DATA 120,169,16,141,20,3,169,192,141,
21,3,88,96,234,234,234,72,138,72,152,72
15 DATA 165,197,197,251,240,81,133,251,2
01,3,208,8,169,48,141,0,193,76,74,192
20 DATA201,4,208,8,169,0,141,0,193,76,74
,192,201,5,208,8,169,16,141,0,193,76,74
25 DATA 192,201,6,208,39,169,32,141,0,19
3,173,141,2,201,1,208,8,173,0,193,105,8
30 DATA141,0,193,162,0,172,0,193,185,1,1
93,157,119,2,232,200,224,8,208,244,134
35 DATA198,104,168,104,170,104,76,49,234

40 FORA=49152TO49267:READB:POKEA,B:NEXT
50 FORA=0TO7:READK$:FORB=1TO8:L=ASC((MID
$(K$,B,1))):IFL=95THENL=13
55 IFL=47THENL=4
60 POKE49409+(A*8)+B,L:NEXT:NEXT:POKE494
09,4:SYS49152
70 DATA"LIST←///"
80 DATA"PRINT///"
90 DATA"RUN←////"
100 DATA"THEN////"
110 DATA"LOAD////"
120 DATA"SAVE////"
130 DATA"VERIFY//"
140 DATA"GOTO////"

READY.
```

5. IRQ clock

The clock routine is updated by the IRQ interrupt which is called by the computer every 50th of a second. The routine used to print line numbers for BASIC is used to print the time (lo byte in X and high byte in A). It is not very good for using when typing in a program as the cursor is always at the top of the screen but it works fine in a program. The syntax to set the clock is as follows:

SYS 28672,hours,minutes.

The clock is in 24 hour format, so remember to enter the time in 24 hour format.

```
PAL (C)1979 BRAD TEMPLETON
2
20:     7000                            .OPT P,00
30:     7000                            *=    $7000
                             ;
                             ;DISPLAYS A CLOCK AT
                             ;TOP LEFT
                             ;OF SCREEN
                             ;
                             ;TO SET TYPE
                             ;
                             ;SYS 24576,HOURS,MINS
                             ;
                             ;SECONDS ASSUMED ZERO
                             ;
150:    7000 20 FD AE                   JSR   $AEFD
160:    7003 20 9E B7                   JSR   $B79E
170:    7006 8A                         TXA
180:    7007 C9 18                      CMP   #24
190:    7009 B0 14                      BCS   IQERR
```

```
200:    700B 8D B7 70              STA    HOUR
                            ;
220:    700E 20 FD AE              JSR    $AEFD
230:    7011 20 9E B7              JSR    $B79E
240:    7014 8A                    TXA
250:    7015 C9 3C                 CMP    #60
260:    7017 B0 06                 BCS    IQERR
270:    7019 8D B8 70              STA    MINUTE
                            ;
290:    701C 4C 22 70              JMP    SETUP
                            ;
310:    701F 4C 48 B2  IQERR       JMP    $B248
                            ;
330:    7022 78        SETUP       SEI
340:    7023 A9 3F                 LDA    #<MAIN
350:    7025 8D 14 03              STA    788
360:    7028 A9 70                 LDA    #>MAIN
370:    702A 8D 15 03              STA    789
380:    702D AD B7 70              LDA    HOUR
400:    7030 AD B8 70              LDA    MINUTE
420:    7033 A9 00                 LDA    #0
430:    7035 8D B9 70              STA    SECOND
450:    7038 A9 00                 LDA    #0
450:    703A 8D BA 70              STA    COUNTER
460:    703D 58                    CLI
470:    703E 60                    RTS
                            ;
                            ;
500:    703F EE BA 70  MAIN        INC    COUNTER
510:    7042 AD BA 70              LDA    COUNTER
520:    7045 C9 3C                 CMP    #60
530:    7047 B0 03                 BCS    CHANGE
                            ;
550:    7049 4C 31 EA              JMP    $EA31
                            ;
570:    704C A9 00     CHANGE      LDA    #0
580:    704E 8D BA 70              STA    COUNTER
                            ;
600:    7051 EE B9 70              INC    SECOND
610:    7054 AD B9 70              LDA    SECOND
620:    7057 C9 3C                 CMP    #60
```

33

```
630:     7Ø59 BØ Ø3                            BCS    MINUTECHANGE
                                        ;
650:     7Ø5B 4C 8D 7Ø                         JMP    PRINT
                                        ;
670:     7Ø5E A9 ØØ          MINUTECHALDA      #Ø
680:     7Ø6Ø 8D B9 7Ø                         STA    SECOND
690:     7Ø63 EE B8 7Ø                         INC    MINUTE
700:     7Ø66 AD B8 7Ø                         LDA    MINUTE
710:     7Ø69 C9 3C                            CMP    #6Ø
720:     7Ø6B BØ Ø3                            BCS    HOURCHANGE
                                        ;
740:     7Ø6D 4C 8D 7Ø                         JMP    PRINT
                                        ;
760:     7Ø7Ø A9 ØØ          HOURCHANGLDA      #Ø
770:     7Ø72 8D B8 7Ø                         STA    MINUTE
780:     7Ø75 EE B7 7Ø                         INC    HOUR
790:     7Ø78 AD B7 7Ø                         LDA    HOUR
800:     7Ø7B C9 18                            CMP    #24
810:     7Ø7D 9Ø ØE                            BCC    PRINT
                                        ;
830:     7Ø7F A9 ØØ                            LDA    #Ø
840:     7Ø81 8D B9 7Ø                         STA    SECOND
850:     7Ø84 8D B8 7Ø                         STA    MINUTE
860:     7Ø87 8D B7 7Ø                         STA    HOUR
870:     7Ø8A 4C 31 EA                         JMP    $EA31
                                        ;
890:     7Ø8D A9 13          PRINT             LDA    #"|
900:     7Ø8F 2Ø D2 FF                         JSR    $FFD2
                                        ;
920:     7Ø92 A9 ØØ                            LDA    #Ø
930:     7Ø94 AE B7 7Ø                         LDX    HOUR
940:     7Ø97 2Ø CD BD                         JSR    $BDCD
                                        ;
960:     7Ø9A A9 3A                            LDA    #":
970:     7Ø9C 2Ø D2 FF                         JSR    $FFD2
                                        ;
990:     7Ø9F A9 ØØ                            LDA    #Ø
1000:    7ØA1 AE B8 7Ø                         LDX    MINUTE
1010:    7ØA4 2Ø CD BD                         JSR    $BDCD
                                        ;
1030:    7ØA7 A9 3A                            LDA    #":
```

```
1040:   70A9 20 D2 FF                JSR   $FFD2
                                *
1060:   70AC A9 00                  LDA   #0
1070:   70AE AE B9 70               LDX   SECOND
1080:   70B1 20 CD BD               JSR   $BDCD
1090:   70B4 4C 31 EA               JMP   $EA31
                                *
1110:   70B7 00       HOUR         .BYT  0
1120:   70B8 00       MINUTE       .BYT  0
1130:   70B9 00       SECOND       .BYT  0
1140:   70BA 00       COUNTER      .BYT  0
]7000-70BB
```

READY.


```
B*
       PC   SR AC XR YR SP
.]97FE 72 00 00 01 F6
.
7000 20 FD AE      JSR  $AEFD
7003 20 9E B7      JSR  $B79E
7006 8A            TXA
7007 C9 18         CMP  #$18
7009 B0 14         BCS  $701F
700B 8D B7 70      STA  $70B7
700E 20 FD AE      JSR  $AEFD
7011 20 9E B7      JSR  $B79E
7014 8A            TXA
7015 C9 3C         CMP  #$3C
7017 B0 06         BCS  $701F
7019 8D B8 70      STA  $70B8
701C 4C 22 70      JMP  $7022
701F 4C 48 B2      JMP  $B248
7022 78            SEI
7023 A9 3F         LDA  #$3F
7025 8D 14 03      STA  $0314
```

```
7028 A9 70        LDA #$70
702A 8D 15 03     STA $0315
702D AD B7 70     LDA $70B7
7030 AD B8 70     LDA $70B8
7033 A9 00        LDA #$00
7035 8D B9 70     STA $70B9
7038 A9 00        LDA #$00
703A 8D BA 70     STA $70BA
703D 58           CLI
703E 60           RTS
703F EE BA 70     INC $70BA
7042 AD BA 70     LDA $70BA
7045 C9 3C        CMP #$3C
7047 B0 03        BCS $704C
7049 4C 31 EA     JMP $EA31
704C A9 00        LDA #$00
704E 8D BA 70     STA $70BA
7051 EE B9 70     INC $70B9
7054 AD B9 70     LDA $70B9
7057 C9 3C        CMP #$3C
7059 B0 03        BCS $705E
705B 4C 8D 70     JMP $708D
705E A9 00        LDA #$00
7060 8D B9 70     STA $70B9
7063 EE B8 70     INC $70B8
7066 AD B8 70     LDA $70B8
7069 C9 3C        CMP #$3C
706B B0 03        BCS $7070
706D 4C 8D 70     JMP $708D
7070 A9 00        LDA #$00
7072 8D B8 70     STA $70B8
7075 EE B7 70     INC $70B7
7078 AD B7 70     LDA $70B7
707B C9 18        CMP #$18
707D 90 0E        BCC $708D
707F A9 00        LDA #$00
7081 8D B9 70     STA $70B9
7084 8D B8 70     STA $70B8
7087 8D B7 70     STA $70B7
708A 4C 31 EA     JMP $EA31
708D A9 13        LDA #$13
```

```
708F 20 D2 FF    JSR *FFD2
7092 A9 00       LDA #$00
7094 AE B7 70    LDX *70B7
7097 20 CD BD    JSR *BDCD
709A A9 3A       LDA #$3A
709C 20 D2 FF    JSR *FFD2
709F A9 00       LDA #$00
70A1 AE B8 70    LDX *70B8
70A4 20 CD BD    JSR *BDCD
70A7 A9 3A       LDA #$3A
70A9 20 D2 FF    JSR *FFD2
70AC A9 00       LDA #$00
70AE AE B9 70    LDX *70B9
70B1 20 CD BD    JSR *BDCD
70B4 4C 31 EA    JMP *EA31
70B7 00          BRK
70B8 00          BRK
70B9 00          BRK
70BA 00          BRK
```

6. Pixel scroll left

The following routine scrolls the screen to the left by one pixel every time that it is called.

To scroll the screen one pixel to the left type SYS 4096.

```
PAL (C)1979 BRAD TEMPLETON
2
20:     1000                        .OPT P,OO
30:     1000                        *=    $1000
40:     1000 AD 16 D0               LDA   53270
50:     1003 29 F8                  AND   #248
60:     1005 18                     CLC
70:     1006 6D 5B 10               ADC   BYTE
80:     1009 8D 16 D0               STA   53270
90:     100C CE 5B 10               DEC   BYTE
100:    100F AD 5B 10               LDA   BYTE
110:    1012 C9 FF                  CMP   #$FF
120:    1014 F0 01                  BEQ   RESET
130:    1016 60                     RTS
140:    1017 AD 16 D0  RESET        LDA   53270
140:    101A 29 F8                  AND   #248
140:    101C 18                     CLC
140:    101D 69 07                  ADC   #7
140:    101F 8D 16 D0               STA   53270
150:    1022 A9 07                  LDA   #7
150:    1024 8D 5B 10               STA   BYTE
160:    1027 20 2B 10               JSR   CHARSCROLL
170:    102A 60                     RTS
180:    102B A9 06     CHARSCROLLDA #6
190:    102D 8D 44 03               STA   $0344
200:    1030 A2 00                  LDX   #0
210:    1032 A0 00                  LDY   #0
220:    1034 BD 01 04  LOOP         LDA   $0401,X
```

```
230:    1037 9D 00 04              STA     $0400,X
240:    103A BD F1 04              LDA     $04F1,X
250:    103D 9D F0 04              STA     $04F0,X
260:    1040 BD E1 05              LDA     $05E1,X
270:    1043 9D E0 05              STA     $05E0,X
280:    1046 BD D1 06              LDA     $06D1,X
290:    1049 9D D0 06              STA     $06D0,X
300:    104C E8                    INX
310:    104D C8                    INY
320:    104E C0 27                 CPY     #$27
330:    1050 D0 E2                 BNE     LOOP
340:    1052 E8                    INX
350:    1053 A0 00                 LDY     #0
360:    1055 CE 44 03              DEC     $0344
370:    1058 D0 DA                 BNE     LOOP
380:    105A 60                    RTS
390:    105B 07          BYTE      .BYTE7
]1000-105C
```

READY.


```
        B*
            PC   SR AC XR YR SP
        .]97FE  72 00 00 01 F6
        .
        1000 AD 16 D0        LDA  $D016
        1003 29 F8           AND  #$F8
        1005 18              CLC
        1006 6D 5B 10        ADC  $105B
        1009 8D 16 D0        STA  $D016
        100C CE 5B 10        DEC  $105B
        100F AD 5B 10        LDA  $105B
        1012 C9 FF           CMP  #$FF
        1014 F0 01           BEQ  $1017
        1016 60              RTS
        1017 AD 16 D0        LDA  $D016
        101A 29 F8           AND  #$F8
```

```
101C  18              CLC
101D  69 07           ADC #$07
101F  8D 16 D0        STA $D016
1022  A9 07           LDA #$07
1024  8D 5B 10        STA $105B
1027  20 2B 10        JSR $102B
102A  60              RTS
102B  A9 06           LDA #$06
102D  8D 44 03        STA $0344
1030  A2 00           LDX #$00
1032  A0 00           LDY #$00
1034  BD 01 04        LDA $0401,X
1037  9D 00 04        STA $0400,X
103A  BD F1 04        LDA $04F1,X
103D  9D F0 04        STA $04F0,X
1040  BD E1 05        LDA $05E1,X
1043  9D E0 05        STA $05E0,X
1046  BD D1 06        LDA $06D1,X
1049  9D D0 06        STA $06D0,X
104C  E8              INX
104D  C8              INY
104E  C0 27           CPY #$27
1050  D0 E2           BNE $1034
1052  E8              INX
1053  A0 00           LDY #$00
1055  CE 44 03        DEC $0344
1058  D0 DA           BNE $1034
105A  60              RTS
105B  07              ???
```

7. Pixel scroll right

The following routine scrolls the screen to the right by one pixel.

To scroll the screen by one pixel to the right type SYS 4096.

```
PAL (C)1979 BRAD TEMPLETON
2
20:     1000                           .OPT P,OO
30:     1000                           *=      $1000
40:     1000 AD 16 DO                  LDA     53270
40:     1003 29 F8                     AND     #248
50:     1005 18                        CLC
50:     1006 6D C9 10                  ADC     BYTE
60:     1009 8D 16 DO                  STA     53270
70:     100C EE C9 10                  INC     BYTE
80:     100F AD C9 10                  LDA     BYTE
90:     1012 C9 08                     CMP     #8
100:    1014 F0 01                     BEQ     RESET
110:    1016 60                        RTS
120:    1017 A9 00        RESET        LDA     #0
120:    1019 8D C9 10                  STA     BYTE
130:    101C AD 16 DO                  LDA     53270
140:    101F 29 F8                     AND     #248
150:    1021 8D 16 DO                  STA     53270
160:    1024 20 28 10                  JSR     CHARSCROLL
170:    1027 60                        RTS
180:    1028 A2 26        CHARSCROLLDX #38
190:    102A BD 00 04 LOOP LDA         1024,X
190:    102D 9D 01 04                  STA     1025,X
200:    1030 BD 28 04                  LDA     1024+40,X
200:    1033 9D 29 04                  STA     1025+40,X
210:    1036 BD 50 04                  LDA     1024+80,X
210:    1039 9D 51 04                  STA     1025+80,X
220:    103C BD 78 04                  LDA     1024+120,X
```

220:	103F	9D	79	04	STA	1025+120,X
230:	1042	BD	A0	04	LDA	1024+160,X
230:	1045	9D	A1	04	STA	1025+160,X
240:	1048	BD	C8	04	LDA	1024+200,X
240:	104B	9D	C9	04	STA	1025+200,X
250:	104E	BD	F0	04	LDA	1024+240,X
250:	1051	9D	F1	04	STA	1025+240,X
260:	1054	BD	18	05	LDA	1024+280,X
260:	1057	9D	19	05	STA	1025+280,X
270:	105A	BD	40	05	LDA	1024+320,X
270:	105D	9D	41	05	STA	1025+320,X
280:	1060	BD	68	05	LDA	1024+360,X
280:	1063	9D	69	05	STA	1025+360,X
290:	1066	BD	90	05	LDA	1024+400,X
290:	1069	9D	91	05	STA	1025+400,X
300:	106C	BD	B8	05	LDA	1024+440,X
300:	106F	9D	B9	05	STA	1025+440,X
310:	1072	BD	E0	05	LDA	1024+480,X
310:	1075	9D	E1	05	STA	1025+480,X
320:	1078	BD	08	06	LDA	1024+520,X
320:	107B	9D	09	06	STA	1025+520,X
330:	107E	BD	30	06	LDA	1024+560,X
330:	1081	9D	31	06	STA	1025+560,X
340:	1084	BD	58	06	LDA	1024+600,X
340:	1087	9D	59	06	STA	1025+600,X
350:	108A	BD	80	06	LDA	1024+640,X
350:	108D	9D	81	06	STA	1025+640,X
360:	1090	BD	A8	06	LDA	1024+680,X
360:	1093	9D	A9	06	STA	1025+680,X
370:	1096	BD	D0	06	LDA	1024+720,X
370:	1099	9D	D1	06	STA	1025+720,X
380:	109C	BD	F8	06	LDA	1024+760,X
380:	109F	9D	F9	06	STA	1025+760,X
390:	10A2	BD	20	07	LDA	1024+800,X
390:	10A5	9D	21	07	STA	1025+800,X
400:	10A8	BD	48	07	LDA	1024+840,X
400:	10AB	9D	49	07	STA	1025+840,X
410:	10AE	BD	70	07	LDA	1024+880,X
410:	10B1	9D	71	07	STA	1025+880,X
420:	10B4	BD	98	07	LDA	1024+920,X
420:	10B7	9D	99	07	STA	1025+920,X
430:	10BA	BD	C0	07	LDA	1024+960,X

```
430:    10BD 9D C1 07           STA   1025+960,X
440:    10C0 CA                 DEX
440:    10C1 E0 FF              CPX   #$FF
440:    10C3 F0 03              BEQ   FIN
440:    10C5 4C 2A 10           JMP   LOOP
450:    10C8 60         FIN     RTS
460:    10C9 00         BYTE    .BYTE0
]1000-10CA
```

READY.

```
B*
    PC   SR AC XR YR SP
.]97FE 72 00 00 01 F6
.
1000 AD 16 D0       LDA  $D016
1003 29 F8          AND  #$F8
1005 18             CLC
1006 6D C9 10       ADC  $10C9
1009 8D 16 D0       STA  $D016
100C EE C9 10       INC  $10C9
100F AD C9 10       LDA  $10C9
1012 C9 08          CMP  #$08
1014 F0 01          BEQ  $1017
1016 60             RTS
1017 A9 00          LDA  #$00
1019 8D C9 10       STA  $10C9
101C AD 16 D0       LDA  $D016
101F 29 F8          AND  #$F8
1021 8D 16 D0       STA  $D016
1024 20 28 10       JSR  $1028
1027 60             RTS
1028 A2 26          LDX  #$26
102A BD 00 04       LDA  $0400,X
102D 9D 01 04       STA  $0401,X
1030 BD 28 04       LDA  $0428,X
```

43

```
1033 9D 29 04        STA $0429,X
1036 BD 50 04        LDA $0450,X
1039 9D 51 04        STA $0451,X
103C BD 78 04        LDA $0478,X
103F 9D 79 04        STA $0479,X
1042 BD A0 04        LDA $04A0,X
1045 9D A1 04        STA $04A1,X
1048 BD C8 04        LDA $04C8,X
104B 9D C9 04        STA $04C9,X
104E BD F0 04        LDA $04F0,X
1051 9D F1 04        STA $04F1,X
1054 BD 18 05        LDA $0518,X
1057 9D 19 05        STA $0519,X
105A BD 40 05        LDA $0540,X
105D 9D 41 05        STA $0541,X
1060 BD 68 05        LDA $0568,X
1063 9D 69 05        STA $0569,X
1066 BD 90 05        LDA $0590,X
1069 9D 91 05        STA $0591,X
106C BD B8 05        LDA $05B8,X
106F 9D B9 05        STA $05B9,X
1072 BD E0 05        LDA $05E0,X
1075 9D E1 05        STA $05E1,X
1078 BD 08 06        LDA $0608,X
107B 9D 09 06        STA $0609,X
107E BD 30 06        LDA $0630,X
1081 9D 31 06        STA $0631,X
1084 BD 58 06        LDA $0658,X
1087 9D 59 06        STA $0659,X
108A BD 80 06        LDA $0680,X
108D 9D 81 06        STA $0681,X
1090 BD A8 06        LDA $06A8,X
1093 9D A9 06        STA $06A9,X
1096 BD D0 06        LDA $06D0,X
1099 9D D1 06        STA $06D1,X
109C BD F8 06        LDA $06F8,X
109F 9D F9 06        STA $06F9,X
10A2 BD 20 07        LDA $0720,X
10A5 9D 21 07        STA $0721,X
10A8 BD 48 07        LDA $0748,X
10AB 9D 49 07        STA $0749,X
```

```
10AE BD 70 07      LDA $0770,X
10B1 9D 71 07      STA $0771,X
10B4 BD 98 07      LDA $0798,X
10B7 9D 99 07      STA $0799,X
10BA BD C0 07      LDA $07C0,X
10BD 9D C1 07      STA $07C1,X
10C0 CA            DEX
10C1 E0 FF         CPX #$FF
10C3 F0 03         BEQ $10C8
10C5 4C 2A 10      JMP $102A
10C8 60            RTS
10C9 00            BRK
```

8. Pixel scroll up

The routine here scrolls the screen up one pixel every time that it is called.

To set up the screen for scrolling type SYS 16384.

To scroll the screen up one pixel type SYS 16398.

```
PAL (C)1979 BRAD TEMPLETON
2
20:     4000                          .OPT P,OO
30:     4000                    *=     $4000
                         ;TO SETUP TYPE
                         ;SYS16384
                         ; TO USE TYPE SYS 16398
70:     4000 AD 11 D0  SETUP    LDA   53265
                         ;USE BEFORE STARTING
80:     4003 29 F7               AND   #247
90:     4005 8D 11 D0            STA   53265
100:    4008 A9 07               LDA   #7
100:    400A 8D 3B 40            STA   BYTE
110:    400D 60                  RTS
                         ; MAIN ROUTINE
130:    400E AD 11 D0            LDA   53265
140:    4011 29 F8               AND   #248
150:    4013 18                  CLC
160:    4014 6D 3B 40            ADC   BYTE
170:    4017 8D 11 D0            STA   53265
180:    401A CE 3B 40            DEC   BYTE
190:    401D AD 3B 40            LDA   BYTE
200:    4020 C9 FF               CMP   #$FF
210:    4022 F0 01               BEQ   RESET
220:    4024 60                  RTS
230:    4025 A9 07      RESET    LDA   #7
230:    4027 8D 3B 40            STA   BYTE
240:    402A AD 11 D0            LDA   53265
```

```
240:    402D 29 F8                  AND   #248
240:    402F 18                     CLC
240:    4030 69 07                  ADC   #7
240:    4032 8D 11 D0                STA   53265
250:    4035 A9 0D                  LDA   #13
260:    4037 20 D2 FF                JSR   $FFD2
270:    403A 60                     RTS
280:    403B 07          BYTE       .BYTE7
]4000-403C
```

READY.

```
B*
        PC  SR AC XR YR SP
.]97FE 72 00 00 01 F6
.
4000 AD 11 D0           LDA  $D011
4003 29 F7              AND  #$F7
4005 8D 11 D0           STA  $D011
4008 A9 07              LDA  #$07
400A 8D 3B 40           STA  $403B
400D 60                 RTS
400E AD 11 D0           LDA  $D011
4011 29 F8              AND  #$F8
4013 18                 CLC
4014 6D 3B 40           ADC  $403B
4017 8D 11 D0           STA  $D011
401A CE 3B 40           DEC  $403B
401D AD 3B 40           LDA  $403B
4020 C9 FF              CMP  #$FF
4022 F0 01              BEQ  $4025
4024 60                 RTS
4025 A9 07              LDA  #$07
4027 8D 3B 40           STA  $403B
402A AD 11 D0           LDA  $D011
402D 29 F8              AND  #$F8
```

```
402F 18          CLC
4030 69 07       ADC #$07
4032 8D 11 D0    STA $D011
4035 A9 0D       LDA #$0D
4037 20 D2 FF    JSR $FFD2
403A 60          RTS
403B 07          ???
```

9. Pixel scroll down

The following routine scrolls the screen down one pixel when it is called. However, due to the way the character scroll works (using the ROM print routine), the top line of the screen is not scrolled. If this routine were coupled with a raster interrupt to suppress the scroll at the top of the screen then this area would stay stationary while the rest would scroll independently.

To set up the screen for scrolling type SYS 16384.

To scroll the screen down one pixel type SYS 16398.

```
PAL (C)1979 BRAD TEMPLETON
2
20:     4000                        .OPT P,00
30:     4000                        *=    $4000
40:     4000 AD 11 D0  SETUP    LDA    53265
                       ; USE SETUP BEFORE
                         STARTING
60:     4003 29 F7              AND    #247
70:     4005 8D 11 D0           STA    53265
80:     4008 A9 00              LDA    #0
80:     400A 8D 4B 40           STA    BYTE
90:     400D 60                 RTS
                       ; MAIN ROUTINE
110:    400E AD 11 D0           LDA    53265
120:    4011 29 F8              AND    #248
130:    4013 18                 CLC
140:    4014 6D 4B 40           ADC    BYTE
150:    4017 8D 11 D0           STA    53265
160:    401A EE 4B 40           INC    BYTE
170:    401D AD 4B 40           LDA    BYTE
180:    4020 C9 08              CMP    #$08
190:    4022 F0 01              BEQ    RESET
200:    4024 60                 RTS
210:    4025 A9 00     RESET    LDA    #0
```

```
210:    4027 8D 4B 40              STA   BYTE
220:    402A AD 11 DØ              LDA   53265
220:    402D 29 F8                 AND   #248
220:    402F 8D 11 DØ              STA   53265
230:    4032 A9 13                 LDA   #"(HOME)"
240:    4034 20 D2 FF              JSR   $FFD2
250:    4037 A9 11                 LDA   #"(CUR DN)"
260:    4039 20 D2 FF              JSR   $FFD2
270:    403C A9 9D                 LDA   #"(CUR L)"
280:    403E 20 D2 FF              JSR   $FFD2
290:    4041 A9 94                 LDA   #"(INST DEL)
300:    4043 20 D2 FF              JSR   $FFD2
310:    4046 A9 80                 LDA   #128
320:    4048 85 DA                 STA   218
330:    404A 60                    RTS
340:    404B 00        BYTE        .BYTE0
]4000-404C
```

READY.


```
B*
     PC   SR AC XR YR SP
.]97FE 72 00 00 01 F6
.
4000 AD 11 DØ      LDA  $D011
4003 29 F7         AND  #$F7
4005 8D 11 DØ      STA  $D011
4008 A9 00         LDA  #$00
400A 8D 4B 40      STA  $404B
400D 60            RTS
400E AD 11 DØ      LDA  $D011
4011 29 F8         AND  #$F8
4013 18            CLC
4014 6D 4B 40      ADC  $404B
4017 8D 11 DØ      STA  $D011
401A EE 4B 40      INC  $404B
401D AD 4B 40      LDA  $404B
```

50

```
4020  C9  08         CMP  #$08
4022  F0  01         BEQ  $4025
4024  60            RTS
4025  A9  00         LDA  #$00
4027  8D  4B  40     STA  $404B
402A  AD  11  D0     LDA  $D011
402D  29  F8         AND  #$F8
402F  8D  11  D0     STA  $D011
4032  A9  13         LDA  #$13
4034  20  D2  FF     JSR  $FFD2
4037  A9  11         LDA  #$11
4039  20  D2  FF     JSR  $FFD2
403C  A9  9D         LDA  #$9D
403E  20  D2  FF     JSR  $FFD2
4041  A9  94         LDA  #$94
4043  20  D2  FF     JSR  $FFD2
4046  A9  80         LDA  #$80
4048  85  DA         STA  $DA
404A  60            RTS
404B  00            BRK
```

10. Colour

This routine allows you to change the screen colour, the border colour, the text colour, extended colours 1, 2 and 3 (or multicolour) in one command.

The syntax is as follows:

SYS 28672,screen colour,border colour,text colour, multi1,multi2,multi3

NB. All parameters must be given.

```
PAL (C)1979 BRAD TEMPLETON
2
20:    7000                           .OPT P,OO
30:    7000                           *=   $7000
                          ;
                          ;ROUTINE TO SET SCREEN
                          ;COLOURS AND BORDER AND
                          ; TEXT,MULTI1,MULTI2
80:    7000 20 FD AE              JSR   $AEFD
90:    7003 20 37 70              JSR   PARAM
100:   7006 8D 21 D0              STA   53281
110:   7009 20 FD AE              JSR   $AEFD
120:   700C 20 37 70              JSR   PARAM
130:   700F 8D 20 D0              STA   53280
                          ;
150:   7012 20 FD AE              JSR   $AEFD
160:   7015 20 37 70              JSR   PARAM
180:   7018 8D 86 02              STA   646
190:   701B 20 FD AE              JSR   $AEFD
200:   701E 20 37 70              JSR   PARAM
220:   7021 8D 22 D0              STA   53282
230:   7024 20 FD AE              JSR   $AEFD
```

```
240:    7027 20 37 70          JSR    PARAM
260:    702A 8D 23 D0          STA    53283
270:    702D 20 FD AE          JSR    *AEFD
280:    7030 20 37 70          JSR    PARAM
300:    7033 8D 24 D0          STA    53284
310:    7036 60               RTS
320:    7037 20 9E B7 PARAM    JSR    *B79E
320:    703A 8A               TXA
330:    703B 60               RTS
340:    703C 4C 48 B2 IQERR    JMP    *B248
17000-703F
```

READY.

```
     B*
         PC  SR AC XR YR SP
     .197FE 72 00 00 01 F6
     .
     7000 20 FD AE      JSR *AEFD
     7003 20 37 70      JSR *7037
     7006 8D 21 D0      STA *D021
     7009 20 FD AE      JSR *AEFD
     700C 20 37 70      JSR *7037
     700F 8D 20 D0      STA *D020
     7012 20 FD AE      JSR *AEFD
     7015 20 37 70      JSR *7037
     7018 8D 86 02      STA *0286
     701B 20 FD AE      JSR *AEFD
     701E 20 37 70      JSR *7037
     7021 8D 22 D0      STA *D022
     7024 20 FD AE      JSR *AEFD
     7027 20 37 70      JSR *7037
     702A 8D 23 D0      STA *D023
     702D 20 FD AE      JSR *AEFD
     7030 20 37 70      JSR *7037
     7033 8D 24 D0      STA *D024
     7036 60            RTS
     7037 20 9E B7      JSR *B79E
     703A 8A            TXA
     703B 60            RTS
     703C 4C 48 B2      JMP *B248
```

11. Copy

This routine allows you to copy the contents of part of or all of the character ROM to a specified part of RAM. This is to make user defined characters easier to set up.

The syntax is SYS 24576,address,no. of pages to copy.

The address is where you want to start your character set at. The number of pages to copy is the number of 256 byte blocks of the ROM to copy down. Only whole numbers are allowed. The character ROM is 16 blocks long. If you specify more than 16 then an illegal quantity error will occur.

e.g. To copy the whole character ROM down to location 8192 type the following:

    SYS 24576,8192,16

or, to copy only the first K of the ROM down to location 12288 type:

    SYS 24576,12288,4

To enable the character set use location 53272 or the change banks routine in this book.

To enable the character set at location 8192 type:

    POKE 53272,24

PAL (C)1979 BRAD TEMPLETON
2

```
20:     6000                          .OPT P,OO
30:     6000                          *=    $6000
                                ;
                                ;ROUTINE TO MOVE
                                ;CHARACTER
                                ;ROM TO SPECIFIED
                                ;LOCATION
                                ;SYNTAX
                                ;
                                ;SYS24576,START,NO OF
                                ;PAGES TO COPY
                                ;WHERE PAGES ARE 256
                                ;BYTES LONG
150:    6000 20 FD AE                 JSR   $AEFD
160:    6003 20 8A AD                 JSR   $AD8A
170:    6006 20 F7 B7                 JSR   $B7F7
180:    6009 A5 14                    LDA   $14
190:    600B 85 FB                    STA   $FB
200:    600D A5 15                    LDA   $15
210:    600F 85 FC                    STA   $FC
                                ;
230:    6011 20 FD AE                 JSR   $AEFD
240:    6014 20 9E B7                 JSR   $B79E
250:    6017 8A                       TXA
260:    6018 C9 11                    CMP   #17
270:    601A 90 03                    BCC   MORE
280:    601C 4C 48 B2                 JMP   $B248
290:    601F 85 FD        MORE        STA   $FD
300:    6021 A9 00                    LDA   #0
310:    6023 8D 5B 60                 STA   TEMP
320:    6026 A0 00                    LDY   #0
330:    6028 A9 00                    LDA   #0
340:    602A 85 FE                    STA   $FE
350:    602C A9 D0                    LDA   #208
360:    602E 85 FF                    STA   $FF
                                ;
375:    6030 A9 00                    LDA   #0
376:    6032 8D 0E DC                 STA   56334
380:    6035 A9 33                    LDA   #51
```

```
390:      6037 85 01            STA  1
400:      6039 B1 FE     LOOP   LDA  ($FE),Y
410:      603B 91 FB            STA  ($FB),Y
420:      603D C8              INY
430:      603E D0 F9            BNE  LOOP
                          ;
450:      6040 EE 5B 60         INC  TEMP
460:      6043 AD 5B 60         LDA  TEMP
470:      6046 C5 FD            CMP  $FD
480:      6048 B0 07            BCS  FINISH
                          ;
500:      604A E6 FC            INC  $FC
510:      604C E6 FF            INC  $FF
520:      604E 4C 39 60         JMP  LOOP
                          ;
540:      6051 A9 37     FINISH LDA  #55
550:      6053 85 01            STA  1
560:      6055 A9 01            LDA  #1
570:      6057 8D 0E DC         STA  56334
580:      605A 60              RTS
590:      605B          TEMP   =    *
]6000-605B
```

READY.

```
          B*
            PC  SR AC XR YR SP
          .]97FE 72 00 00 01 F6
          .
          6000 20 FD AE     JSR  $AEFD
          6003 20 8A AD     JSR  $AD8A
          6006 20 F7 B7     JSR  $B7F7
          6009 A5 14        LDA  $14
          600B 85 FB        STA  $FB
          600D A5 15        LDA  $15
          600F 85 FC        STA  $FC
```

```
6011 20 FD AE    JSR $AEFD
6014 20 9E B7    JSR $B79E
6017 8A          TXA
6018 C9 11       CMP #$11
601A 90 03       BCC $601F
601C 4C 48 B2    JMP $B248
601F 85 FD       STA $FD
6021 A9 00       LDA #$00
6023 8D 5B 60    STA $605B
6026 A0 00       LDY #$00
6028 A9 00       LDA #$00
602A 85 FE       STA $FE
602C A9 D0       LDA #$D0
602E 85 FF       STA $FF
6030 A9 00       LDA #$00
6032 8D 0E DC    STA $DC0E
6035 A9 33       LDA #$33
6037 85 01       STA $01
6039 B1 FE       LDA ($FE),Y
603B 91 FB       STA ($FB),Y
603D C8          INY
603E D0 F9       BNE $6039
6040 EE 5B 60    INC $605B
6043 AD 5B 60    LDA $605B
6046 C5 FD       CMP $FD
6048 B0 07       BCS $6051
604A E6 FC       INC $FC
604C E6 FF       INC $FF
604E 4C 39 60    JMP $6039
6051 A9 37       LDA #$37
6053 85 01       STA $01
6055 A9 01       LDA #$01
6057 8D 0E DC    STA $DC0E
605A 60          RTS
```
.

12. Sprite/char

If you are using sprites in a program the time will come when you want to find what character the sprite is under or over. You can see which one, but the computer cannot. Commodore kindly made it possible for the video chip to detect if it has hit a character or not, but not to detect which one. The following program does this. It is written to detect the charcter under sprite 0. To find out which character it is, use SYS 16384 from Basic or JSR $4000 from machine code. The character code is returned in location 828 ($033C), so to find the character execute the routine and PEEK or LDA(X or Y) location 828 ($033C)

No doubt you will want to check which character is under a different sprite than sprite 0. Rather than listing 8 programs, one for each sprite, here is a list of what to change to make it work for any sprite:

1. Change the first line from LDA $D000 to LDA $ hex location of 'X' coordinate of the sprite that you want to test.

2. Change the line at address $400A to CMP #$ bit value of sprite to be tested (sprite 0 = 1 through to sprite 7 = 128).

3. Change the line at address $400E to LDX $ hex location of 'X' coordinate of the sprite to be tested.

4. Change the line at address $4011 to LDA $ hex location of 'Y' coordinate of sprite to be tested.

5. Change the line at address $4032 to CMP #$ bit value of sprite to be tested (as in 2).

The routine checks which character is under the top left 8 bytes of the sprite (going down). i.e.

```
1 2 3
1 2 3
1 2 3
1 2 3
1 2 3
1 2 3
1 2 3
1 2 3
```
and so on ...

It checks the character under the 1s in the above diagram, but this can be altered by changing two bytes in the program as follows:

The line at location $4004 is SBC #$18. The number after the SBC must never be less than $18 (24), but if you add one to this value for every bit across the sprite then you can alter where on the horizontal the routine will check. (This number must never exceed $30 (48) if the sprite is not expanded in the 'X' direction or $60 (96) if expanded.) Remember that as the sprite is expanded each dot on the sprite is 2 dots wide, therefore you will need to multiply the amount greater than $18 by two and add it to $18.

e.g. to get the routine to check for the rightmost 8 bits of an unexpanded sprite, make the line SBC #$30.

Or, to get the routine to check for the 7th to the 15th bit across in an expanded sprite, make the line SBC #(24 + 7*2) which is SBC #$26.

To alter where the routine checks on the vertical change the line at address $4015 (SBC #$3A). The rules for changing are the same as for the 'X' direction. If the sprite is unexpanded in the 'Y' direction then the value is $3A + the byte down. If the sprite is expanded then the value is $3A + 2* the byte down. The value must never be less than $3A and if the sprite is unexpanded no greater than $4F (79) or if the sprite is expanded no greater than $64 (100) for the routine.

e.g. to make the routine check for the bottom 8 bytes of the sprite when it is unexpanded the line is SBC #$47.

or, to make the routine check for the 10th to the 18th byte down in an expanded sprite the line is SBC #$3A + 2*10 which is SBC #$4E

```
PAL (C)1979 BRAD TEMPLETON
2
20:     4000                       .OPT  P,00
30:     4000                       *=    $4000
40:     4000 AD 00 D0               LDA   53248
50:     4003 38                     SEC
50:     4004 E9 18                  SBC   #24
50:     4006 AA                     TAX
60:     4007 AD 10 D0               LDA   53264
60:     400A C9 01                  CMP   #1
60:     400C D0 03                  BNE   MORE
70:     400E AE 00 D0               LDX   53248
80:     4011 AD 01 D0 MORE          LDA   53249
80:     4014 38                     SEC
80:     4015 E9 3A                  SBC   #58
80:     4017 A8                     TAY
90:     4018 8E 98 40               STX   X1STORE ;X1
100:    401B 8C 9A 40               STY   Y1STORE ;Y1
110:    401E 98                     TYA
120:    401F 4A                     LSR   A
120:    4020 4A                     LSR   A
120:    4021 4A                     LSR   A ;Y2=Y1/8
130:    4022 18                     CLC
130:    4023 69 01                  ADC   #1
130:    4025 8D 9B 40               STA   Y2STORE
140:    4028 8A                     TXA
150:    4029 4A                     LSR   A
150:    402A 4A                     LSR   A
150:    402B 4A                     LSR   A ;X2=X2/8
160:    402C 8D 99 40               STA   X2STORE
170:    402F AD 10 D0               LDA   53264
170:    4032 C9 01                  CMP   #1
170:    4034 D0 09                  BNE   MORE1
180:    4036 AD 99 40               LDA   X2STORE
190:    4039 18                     CLC
```

```
190:    403A 69 1D              ADC     #29
200:    403C 8D 99 40           STA     X2STORE
210:    403F AD 9B 40 MORE1     LDA     Y2STORE
220:    4042 8D 96 40           STA     NUMBER1
230:    4045 A9 28              LDA     #40
240:    4047 8D 97 40           STA     NUMBER2
250:    404A 20 79 40           JSR     MULTIPLY
260:    404D AD 99 40           LDA     X2STORE
270:    4050 6D 94 40           ADC     RESULT
280:    4053 8D 94 40           STA     RESULT
290:    4056 AD 95 40           LDA     RESULT+1
300:    4059 69 00              ADC     #0
310:    405B 8D 95 40           STA     RESULT+1
320:    405E AD 95 40           LDA     RESULT+1
330:    4061 18                 CLC
340:    4062 69 04              ADC     #4
350:    4064 8D 95 40           STA     RESULT+1
                        ; CHARACTER IN LOCATION
                        ;IN LOCS RESULT AND RESULT+1
380:    4067 AD 94 40           LDA     RESULT
380:    406A 85 FB              STA     $FB
390:    406C AD 95 40           LDA     RESULT+1
390:    406F 85 FC              STA     $FC
400:    4071 A0 00              LDY     #0
410:    4073 B1 FB              LDA     ($FB),Y
420:    4075 8D 3C 03           STA     828
430:    4078 60                 RTS
440:    4079 A9 00     MULTIPLY LDA     #0
450:    407B 8D 94 40           STA     RESULT
460:    407E A2 08              LDX     #8
470:    4080 4E 96 40 LOOP      LSR     NUMBER1
480:    4083 90 04              BCC     NOADD
490:    4085 18                 CLC
500:    4086 6D 97 40           ADC     NUMBER2
510:    4089 6A       NOADD     ROR     A
520:    408A 6E 94 40           ROR     RESULT
530:    408D CA                 DEX
540:    408E D0 F0              BNE     LOOP
550:    4090 8D 95 40           STA     RESULT+1
560:    4093 60                 RTS
                        ;
```

61

```
580:    4094 00 00    RESULT    .WORD0
590:    4096 00        NUMBER1   .BYTE0
600:    4097 00        NUMBER2   .BYTE0
610:    4098 00        X1STORE   .BYTE0
620:    4099 00        X2STORE   .BYTE0
630:    409A 00        Y1STORE   .BYTE0
640:    409B 00        Y2STORE   .BYTE0
]4000-409C

READY.
```

```
B*
    PC   SR AC XR YR SP
.197FE 72 00 00 01 F6
.
4000 AD 00 D0      LDA *D000
4003 38            SEC
4004 E9 18         SBC #*18
4006 AA            TAX
4007 AD 10 D0      LDA *D010
400A C9 01         CMP #*01
400C D0 03         BNE *4011
400E AE 00 D0      LDX *D000
4011 AD 01 D0      LDA *D001
4014 38            SEC
4015 E9 3A         SBC #*3A
4017 A8            TAY
4018 8E 98 40      STX *4098
401B 8C 9A 40      STY *409A
401E 98            TYA
401F 4A            LSR
4020 4A            LSR
4021 4A            LSR
4022 18            CLC
4023 69 01         ADC #*01
4025 8D 9B 40      STA *409B
```

```
4028 8A              TXA
4029 4A              LSR
402A 4A              LSR
402B 4A              LSR
402C 8D 99 40        STA $4099
402F AD 10 D0        LDA $D010
4032 C9 01           CMP #$01
4034 D0 09           BNE $403F
4036 AD 99 40        LDA $4099
4039 18              CLC
403A 69 1D           ADC #$1D
403C 8D 99 40        STA $4099
403F AD 9B 40        LDA $409B
4042 8D 96 40        STA $4096
4045 A9 28           LDA #$28
4047 8D 97 40        STA $4097
404A 20 79 40        JSR $4079
404D AD 99 40        LDA $4099
4050 6D 94 40        ADC $4094
4053 8D 94 40        STA $4094
4056 AD 95 40        LDA $4095
4059 69 00           ADC #$00
405B 8D 95 40        STA $4095
405E AD 95 40        LDA $4095
4061 18              CLC
4062 69 04           ADC #$04
4064 8D 95 40        STA $4095
4067 AD 94 40        LDA $4094
406A 85 FB           STA $FB
406C AD 95 40        LDA $4095
406F 85 FC           STA $FC
4071 A0 00           LDY #$00
4073 B1 FB           LDA ($FB),Y
4075 8D 3C 03        STA $033C
4078 60              RTS
4079 A9 00           LDA #$00
407B 8D 94 40        STA $4094
407E A2 08           LDX #$08
4080 4E 96 40        LSR $4096
4083 90 04           BCC $4089
4085 18              CLC
```

```
4086 6D 97 40    ADC $4097
4089 6A          ROR
408A 6E 94 40    ROR $4094
408D CA          DEX
408E DØ FØ       BNE $4080
4090 8D 95 40    STA $4095
4093 60          RTS
4094 ØØ          BRK
4095 ØØ          BRK
4096 ØØ          BRK
4097 ØØ          BRK
4098 ØØ          BRK
4099 ØØ          BRK
409A ØØ          BRK
409B ØØ          BRK
```

13. Doke

The following routine allows you to POKE a 16 bit number into two consecutive locations . This could be to change a RAM vector. It replaces the following line of Basic code:

a = number: hi = int(a/256): lo = (a-number)*256: poke address,lo:pokeaddress + 1,hi

To use the routine type SYS 960,address,number.

e.g. to change the output character routine to point to your own routine at 828 (as in the list alter routine later) type SYS 960,806,828.

```
PAL (C)1979 BRAD TEMPLETON
2
20:      03C0                        .OPT P,00
30:      03C0                        *=   960
                          ;
                          ; DOKE ROUTINE
                          ;
                          ;SYNTAX SYS 960,
                          ;ADDRESS,VALUE
                          ; EG SYS16384,788,16384
                          ;
110:     03C0 20 FD AE              JSR  $AEFD
120:     03C3 20 8A AD              JSR  $AD8A
130:     03C6 20 F7 B7              JSR  $B7F7
                          ;
150:     03C9 A5 14                 LDA  $14
160:     03CB 85 FB                 STA  $FB
170:     03CD A5 15                 LDA  $15
180:     03CF 85 FC                 STA  $FC
                          ;
```

```
200:    03D1 20 FD AE          JSR    $AEFD
210:    03D4 20 8A AD          JSR    $AD8A
220:    03D7 20 F7 B7          JSR    $B7F7
                         |
240:    03DA A0 00            LDY    #0
250:    03DC A5 14            LDA    $14
260:    03DE 91 FB            STA    ($FB),Y
270:    03E0 A0 01            LDY    #1
280:    03E2 A5 15            LDA    $15
290:    03E4 91 FB            STA    ($FB),Y
                         |
310:    03E6 60              RTS
]03C0-03E7

READY.




B*
     PC   SR AC XR YR SP
.]97FE 72 00 00 01 F6
.
03C0 20 FD AE      JSR $AEFD
03C3 20 8A AD      JSR $AD8A
03C6 20 F7 B7      JSR $B7F7
03C9 A5 14         LDA $14
03CB 85 FB         STA $FB
03CD A5 15         LDA $15
03CF 85 FC         STA $FC
03D1 20 FD AE      JSR $AEFD
03D4 20 8A AD      JSR $AD8A
03D7 20 F7 B7      JSR $B7F7
03DA A0 00         LDY #$00
03DC A5 14         LDA $14
03DE 91 FB         STA ($FB),Y
03E0 A0 01         LDY #$01
03E2 A5 15         LDA $15
03E4 91 FB         STA ($FB),Y
03E6 60            RTS
```

14. Deek

This routine is complementary to Doke. It allows you to read the contents of two consecutive locations in memory. It replaces the following line of Basic code:

PRINT PEEK(ADDRESS) + 256*PEEK(ADDRESS + 1)

The routine cannot create a variable (e.g. a = Deek (address) is not possible).

The syntax for the routine is as follows:

SYS 828,address

```
PAL (C)1979 BRAD TEMPLETON
2
20:    033C                      .OPT P,00
30:    033C                      *=    828
                        ;
                        ; SIMULATED DEEK
                        ; FUNCTION
                        ;ONLY USED TO PRINT
                        ;THE VALUE
                        ;IN TWO CONSECUTIVE
                        ;
                        ;LOCATIONS IN 16 BIT
                        ;FORMAT
                        ;SYNTAX
                        ;
                        ;SYS828,ADDRESS
                        ;
                        ;EG. SYS828,788
                        ;
                        ;WILL RETURN 59953
                        ;
```

```
210:     Ø33C 20 FD AE              JSR    $AEFD
220:     Ø33F 20 8A AD              JSR    $AD8A
230:     Ø342 20 F7 B7              JSR    $B7F7
                                ;
250:     Ø345 A5 14                LDA    $14
260:     Ø347 85 FB                STA    $FB
270:     Ø349 A5 15                LDA    $15
280:     Ø34B 85 FC                STA    $FC
                                ;
300:     Ø34D AØ ØØ                LDY    #Ø
310:     Ø34F B1 FB                LDA    ($FB),Y
320:     Ø351 C8                   INY
330:     Ø352 AA                   TAX
340:     Ø353 B1 FB                LDA    ($FB),Y
                                ;
360:     Ø355 4C CD BD             JMP    $BDCD
                                ;
JØ33C-Ø358

READY.



         B*
            PC   SR AC XR YR SP
         .J97FE 72 ØØ ØØ Ø1 F6
            .
         Ø33C 20 FD AE      JSR $AEFD
         Ø33F 20 8A AD      JSR $AD8A
         Ø342 20 F7 B7      JSR $B7F7
         Ø345 A5 14         LDA $14
         Ø347 85 FB         STA $FB
         Ø349 A5 15         LDA $15
         Ø34B 85 FC         STA $FC
         Ø34D AØ ØØ         LDY #$ØØ
         Ø34F B1 FB         LDA ($FB),Y
         Ø351 C8            INY
         Ø352 AA            TAX
         Ø353 B1 FB         LDA ($FB),Y
         Ø355 4C CD BD      JMP $BDCD
```

15. 3 channel IRQ tune

The following routine will play a tune independently of the other things that the computer is doing.

The routine is enabled by SYS 24576 and can be stopped with run/stop and restore.

The data for the tune is held in the tunetable in the PAL listing and from location $6074 onwards in the disassembly.

```
PAL  (C)1979 BRAD TEMPLETON
2
20:      6000                              .OPT  P,00
30:      6000                              *=    $6000

40:      6000 78                           SEI
40:      6001 A9 32                        LDA   #<MAI
N
40:      6003 8D 14 03                     STA   788
40:      6006 A9 60                        LDA   #>MAI
N
40:      6008 8D 15 03                     STA   789
40:      600B A9 0F                        LDA   #15
40:      600D 8D 18 D4                     STA   54296

50:      6010 A9 13                        LDA   #19
50:      6012 8D 04 D4                     STA   54276

50:      6015 A9 40                        LDA   #64
50:      6017 8D 05 D4                     STA   54277

50:      601A 8D 06 D4                     STA   54278

50:      601D 8D 0C D4                     STA   54284
```

69

```
50:        6020 8D ØD D4              STA    54285

52:        6023 A9 21                LDA    #33
52:        6025 8D ØB D4              STA    54283

55:        6028 A9 ØØ                LDA    #Ø
55:        602A 85 FB                STA    251
55:        602C 85 FC                STA    252
55:        602E 85 FD                STA    253
55:        6030 58                   CLI
55:        6031 60                   RTS
                              ;
70:        6032 A6 FB        MAIN    LDX    251
70:        6034 A4 FC                LDY    252
70:        6036
80:        6036 BD 74 60              LDA    TUNE,
X
90:        6039 8D ØØ D4              STA    54272

95:        603C BD A6 60              LDA    TUNE1
-2,X
95:        603F 8D Ø7 D4              STA    54279

95:        6042 BD A7 60              LDA    TUNE1
-1,X
95:        6045 8D Ø8 D4              STA    54280

100:       6048 BD 75 60              LDA    TUNE+
1,X
110:       604B 8D Ø1 D4              STA    54273

120:       604E A5 FD                LDA    253
130:       6050 C9 ØA                CMP    #10
140:       6052 BØ Ø5                BCS    NEXDE
LAY
150:       6054 E6 FD                INC    253
150:       6056 4C 31 EA              JMP    $EA31

160:       6059 A9 ØØ        NEXDELAY LDA    #Ø
160:       605B 85 FD                STA    253
160:       605D E8                   INX
```

```
160:     605E E8                        INX
160:     605F C8                        INY
160:     6060 86 FB                     STX    251
160:     6062 84 FC                     STY    252
160:     6064 E0 30                     CPX    #48
160:     6066 B0 03                     BCS    RE
160:     6068 4C 31 EA                  JMP    $EA31

165:     606B A2 00      RE            LDX    #0
165:     606D 85 FB                     STA    251
165:     606F 85 FC                     STA    252
165:     6071 4C 31 EA                  JMP    $EA31


1000:    6074 C6 2D 00 TUNE           .BYT 198,4
5,0,0,198,45,52,43,126,38,0,0,126,38
1010:    6082 4B 22 7E                .BYT 75,34
,126,38,75,34,141,30,214,28,0,0
1015:    608E D6 1C 8D                .BYT 214,2
8,141,30,75,34,227,22
1020:    6096 B1 19 8D                .BYT 177,2
5,141,30,214,28,177,25,227,22
1030:    60A0 00 00 00                .BYT 0,0,0
,0,0,0,0,0
1050:    60A8 72 0B 00 TUNE1          .BYT 114,1
1,0,0,114,11,205,10,159,9,0,0,159,9
1060:    60B6 93 08 9F                .BYT 147,8
,159,9,147,8,163,7,53,7,0,0
1070:    60C2 35 07 A3                .BYT 53,7,
163,7,147,8,185,5
1080:    60CA 6C 06 A3                .BYT 108,6
,163,7,53,7,108,6,185,5
1090:    60D4 00 00 00                .BYT 0,0,0
,0,0,0,0,0
16000-60DC

READY.
```

71

```
B*
     PC  SR AC XR YR SP
.;97FE 72 00 00 01 F6
.
6000 78              SEI
6001 A9 32           LDA #$32
6003 8D 14 03        STA $0314
6006 A9 60           LDA #$60
6008 8D 15 03        STA $0315
600B A9 0F           LDA #$0F
600D 8D 18 D4        STA $D418
6010 A9 13           LDA #$13
6012 8D 04 D4        STA $D404
6015 A9 40           LDA #$40
6017 8D 05 D4        STA $D405
601A 8D 06 D4        STA $D406
601D 8D 0C D4        STA $D40C
6020 8D 0D D4        STA $D40D
6023 A9 21           LDA #$21
6025 8D 0B D4        STA $D40B
6028 A9 00           LDA #$00
602A 85 FB           STA $FB
602C 85 FC           STA $FC
602E 85 FD           STA $FD
6030 58              CLI
6031 60              RTS
6032 A6 FB           LDX $FB
6034 A4 FC           LDY $FC
6036 BD 74 60        LDA $6074,X
6039 8D 00 D4        STA $D400
603C BD A6 60        LDA $60A6,X
603F 8D 07 D4        STA $D407
6042 BD A7 60        LDA $60A7,X
6045 8D 08 D4        STA $D408
6048 BD 75 60        LDA $6075,X
604B 8D 01 D4        STA $D401
604E A5 FD           LDA $FD
6050 C9 0A           CMP #$0A
6052 B0 05           BCS $6059
6054 E6 FD           INC $FD
6056 4C 31 EA        JMP $EA31
```

```
6059 A9 00          LDA #$00
605B 85 FD          STA $FD
605D E8             INX
605E E8             INX
605F C8             INY
6060 86 FB          STX $FB
6062 84 FC          STY $FC
6064 E0 30          CPX #$30
6066 B0 03          BCS $606B
6068 4C 31 EA       JMP $EA31
606B A2 00          LDX #$00
606D 85 FB          STA $FB
606F 85 FC          STA $FC
6071 4C 31 EA       JMP $EA31
6074 C6 2D          DEC $2D
6076 00             BRK
6077 00             BRK
6078 C6 2D          DEC $2D
```

```
.
.:6074 C6 2D 00 00 C6 2D 34 2B
.:607C 7E 26 00 00 7E 26 4B 22
.:6084 7E 26 4B 22 8D 1E D6 1C
.:608C 00 00 D6 1C 8D 1E 4B 22
.:6094 E3 16 B1 19 8D 1E D6 1C
.:609C B1 19 E3 16 00 00 00 00
.:60A4 00 00 00 00 72 0B 00 00
.:60AC 72 0B CD 0A 9F 09 00 00
.:60B4 9F 09 93 08 9F 09 93 08
.:60BC A3 07 35 07 00 00 35 07
.:60C4 A3 07 93 08 B9 05 6C 06
.:60CC A3 07 35 07 6C 06 B9 05
.:60D4 00 00 00 00 00 00 00 00
```

73

16. List alter

The following routine lets you list a program in a specified column width. I have used it to list the Supermon loader in a width suitable for a book page.

To use this routine type SYS 828,number of columns.

```
PAL (C) 1979 BRAD TEMPLETON
2
20:    033C                              .OPT  P,OO
30:    033C                              *=    $033C
40:    033C                 IBSOUT       =     $0326
50:    033C 20 FD AE                     JSR   $AEFD
60:    033F 20 9E B7                     JSR   $B79E
70:    0342 8E 77 03                     STX   COLUMN
80:    0345 AD 26 03                     LDA   IBSOUT
90:    0348 8D 78 03                     STA   OLDOUT
100:   034B AD 27 03                     LDA   IBSOUT+1
110:   034E 8D 79 03                     STA   OLDOUT+1
120:   0351 A9 5C                        LDA   #<MAIN
130:   0353 8D 26 03                     STA   IBSOUT
140:   0356 A9 03                        LDA   #>MAIN
150:   0358 8D 27 03                     STA   IBSOUT+1
160:   035B 60                           RTS
                                   ;
180:   035C C9 0D        MAIN          CMP   #13
190:   035E F0 08                      BEQ   DOCR
200:   0360 CE 7A 03                   DEC   COUNT
210:   0363 D0 0B                      BNE   NADDCR
220:   0365 20 74 03                   JSR   NEWPRT
230:   0368 AD 77 03     DOCR          LDA   COLUMN
240:   036B 8D 7A 03                   STA   COUNT
250:   036E A9 0D                      LDA   #13
260:   0370 20 74 03     NADDCR        JSR   NEWPRT
```

```
270:      0373 60                    RTS
280:      0374 6C 78 03  NEWPRT  JMP    (OLDOUT)
290:      0377 50        COLUMN  .BYT 80
300:      0378           OLDOUT  =      *
310:      0378           COUNT   =      OLDOUT+2
]033C-0378
```

READY.

```
B*
       PC  SR AC XR YR SP
.]97FE 72 00 00 01 F6
.
033C 20 FD AE      JSR $AEFD
033F 20 9E B7      JSR $B79E
0342 8E 77 03      STX $0377
0345 AD 26 03      LDA $0326
0348 8D 78 03      STA $0378
034B AD 27 03      LDA $0327
034E 8D 79 03      STA $0379
0351 A9 5C         LDA #$5C
0353 8D 26 03      STA $0326
0356 A9 03         LDA #$03
0358 8D 27 03      STA $0327
035B 60            RTS
035C C9 0D         CMP #$0D
035E F0 08         BEQ $0368
0360 CE 7A 03      DEC $037A
0363 D0 0B         BNE $0370
0365 20 74 03      JSR $0374
0368 AD 77 03      LDA $0377
036B 8D 7A 03      STA $037A
036E A9 0D         LDA #$0D
0370 20 74 03      JSR $0374
0373 60            RTS
0374 6C 78 03      JMP ($0378)
0377 50 00         BVC $0379
```

17. Old

This routine allows a program accidentally newed to be recovered. It also works after a SYS 64738 or SYS 58260 (cold or warm start). If the old routine is not in memory when you need it, do not worry: it can be loaded in after the new and executed and the program will still be recovered.

To use type SYS 300.

To load into memory after a new type LOAD"OLD",8,1 (or LOAD"OLD",1,1) and then SYS 300.

```
PAL  (C)1979  BRAD TEMPLETON
2
20:     012C                          .OPT  P,00
30:     012C                          *=    300
                             ;OLD ROUTINE
50:     012C A9 FF                     LDA   #$FF
60:     012E A0 01                     LDY   #1
70:     0130 91 2B                     STA   ($2B),8Y
80:     0132 20 33 A5                  JSR   $A533
90:     0135 A5 22                     LDA   $22
100:    0137 18                        CLC
110:    0138 69 02                     ADC   #2
110:    013A 85 2D                     STA   $2D
120:    013C A5 23                     LDA   $23
130:    013E 69 00                     ADC   #0
140:    0140 85 2E                     STA   $2E
150:    0142 4C 5E A6                  JMP   $A65E
]012C-0145
```

READY.

B*
```
   PC   SR AC XR YR SP
.|97FE 72 00 00 01 F6
.
.
```

B*
```
   PC   SR AC XR YR SP
.|97FE 72 00 00 01 F6
.
012C A9 FF          LDA #$FF
012E A0 01          LDY #$01
0130 91 2B          STA ($2B),Y
0132 20 33 A5       JSR $A533
0135 A5 22          LDA $22
0137 18             CLC
0138 69 02          ADC #$02
013A 85 2D          STA $2D
013C A5 23          LDA $23
013E 69 00          ADC #$00
0140 85 2E          STA $2E
0142 4C 5E A6       JMP $A65E
.
```

18. Graph

This routine is the graph (or high res) command. It turns on the high res screen which is located at 24576 and the colour memory at 16384. It does not clear the screen.

To use type SYS 49152.

```
PAL (C)1979 BRAD TEMPLETON
2
20:      C000                            .OPT P,00
30:      C000                            *=   *C000
                               ;
                               ;GRAPH FUNCTION 26
                               ;
70:      C000 A9 16                      LDA  #$16
90:      C002 8D 00 DD                   STA  56576
                               ;CHANGE  BLOCK   .
                               ;
110:     C005 A9 08                      LDA  #8
120:     C007 8D 18 D0                   STA  53272
                               ;
140:     C00A AD 11 D0                   LDA  53265
140:     C00D 09 20                      ORA  #32
140:     C00F 8D 11 D0                   STA  53265
150:     C012 60                         RTS
]C000-C013

READY.
```

```
B*
     PC   SR AC XR YR SP
.197FE 72 00 00 01 F6
.
C000 A9 16           LDA #$16
C002 8D 00 DD        STA $DD00
C005 A9 08           LDA #$08
C007 8D 18 D0        STA $D018
C00A AD 11 D0        LDA $D011
C00D 09 20           ORA #$20
C00F 8D 11 D0        STA $D011
C012 60              RTS
```

19. NRM

This is the complementary routine to graph. It turns the high res screen off and returns to the normal text screen.

To use type SYS 49174.

```
PAL (C)1979 BRAD TEMPLETON
2
20:      C016                              .OPT  P,00
30:      C016                              *=    $C016
                              ;NORM COMMAND
50:      C016 A9 15                        LDA   #21
60:      C018 8D 18 D0                     STA   53272
70:      C01B A9 1B                        LDA   #27
80:      C01D 8D 11 D0                     STA   53265
90:      C020 A9 17                        LDA   #23
100:     C022 8D 00 DD                     STA   56576
110:     C025 60                           RTS
]C016-C026

READY.


            B*
              PC  SR AC XR YR SP
            .;97FE 72 00 00 01 F6
            .
            C016 A9 15           LDA #$15
            C018 8D 18 D0        STA $D018
            C01B A9 1B           LDA #$1B
            C01D 8D 11 D0        STA $D011
            C020 A9 17           LDA #$17
            C022 8D 00 DD        STA $DD00
            C025 60              RTS
```

20. CLG

This routine clears the high res screen. Two parameters are required. The first defines the drawing colour and the second the background colour. Both are values between 0 and 15 and are the same as the usual text colours.

To use type SYS 49190, drawing colour, background colour.

```
PAL (C)1979 BRAD TEMPLETON
2
20:     C026                        .OPT P,OO
30:     C026                        *=    $C026
                            ; CLG COMMAND
50:     C026 20 FD AE               JSR   $AEFD
60:     C029 20 8A AD               JSR   $AD8A
70:     C02C 20 F7 B7               JSR   $B7F7
80:     C02F A5 15                  LDA   $15
80:     C031 F0 03                  BEQ   MORE
80:     C033 4C 48 B2               JMP   $B248
90:     C036 A5 14      MORE        LDA   $14
90:     C038 8D 85 C0               STA   FIN
100:    C03B 20 FD AE               JSR   $AEFD
110:    C03E 20 8A AD               JSR   $AD8A
120:    C041 20 F7 B7               JSR   $B7F7
130:    C044 A5 15                  LDA   $15
130:    C046 F0 03                  BEQ   MORE1
130:    C048 4C 48 B2               JMP   $B248
140:    C04B A5 14      MORE1       LDA   $14
140:    C04D 0A                     ASL   A
140:    C04E 0A                     ASL   A
140:    C04F 0A                     ASL   A
140:    C050 0A                     ASL   A
140:    C051 0D 85 C0               ORA   FIN
140:    C054 8D 85 C0               STA   FIN
```

```
150:    CØ57 A9 ØØ                LDA    #Ø
150:    CØ59 85 FB                STA    $FB
16Ø:    CØ5B A9 6Ø                LDA    #96
16Ø:    CØ5D 85 FC                STA    $FC
17Ø:    CØ5F AØ ØØ                LDY    #Ø
18Ø:    CØ61 A9 ØØ                LDA    #Ø
19Ø:    CØ63 91 FB      LOOP      STA    ($FB),Y
2ØØ:    CØ65 C8                   INY
21Ø:    CØ66 DØ FB                BNE    LOOP
22Ø:    CØ68 E6 FC                INC    $FC
23Ø:    CØ6A A6 FC                LDX    $FC
24Ø:    CØ6C EØ 8Ø                CPX    #128
25Ø:    CØ6E DØ F3                BNE    LOOP
26Ø:    CØ7Ø AD 85 CØ             LDA    FIN
27Ø:    CØ73 A2 ØØ                LDX    #Ø
28Ø:    CØ75 9D ØØ 4Ø  LOOP1     STA    $4ØØØ,X
29Ø:    CØ78 9D ØØ 41             STA    $41ØØ,X
3ØØ:    CØ7B 9D ØØ 42             STA    $42ØØ,X
31Ø:    CØ7E 9D ØØ 43             STA    $43ØØ,X
32Ø:    CØ81 E8                   INX
32Ø:    CØ82 DØ F1                BNE    LOOP1
32Ø:    CØ84 6Ø                   RTS
33Ø:    CØ85           FIN        =      *
]CØ26-CØ85
```

READY.

```
        B*
            PC   SR AC XR YR SP
        .)97FE 72 ØØ ØØ Ø1 F6
        .
        CØ26 2Ø FD AE      JSR    $AEFD
        CØ29 2Ø 8A AD      JSR    $AD8A
        CØ2C 2Ø F7 B7      JSR    $B7F7
        CØ2F A5 15         LDA    $15
        CØ31 FØ Ø3         BEQ    $CØ36
        CØ33 4C 48 B2      JMP    $B248
        CØ36 A5 14         LDA    $14
```

```
C038 8D 85 CØ      STA $C085
CØ3B 20 FD AE      JSR $AEFD
CØ3E 20 8A AD      JSR $AD8A
CØ41 20 F7 B7      JSR $B7F7
CØ44 A5 15         LDA $15
CØ46 FØ Ø3         BEQ $C04B
CØ48 4C 48 B2      JMP $B248
CØ4B A5 14         LDA $14
CØ4D ØA            ASL
CØ4E ØA            ASL
CØ4F ØA            ASL
CØ50 ØA            ASL
CØ51 ØD 85 CØ      ORA $C085
CØ54 8D 85 CØ      STA $C085
CØ57 A9 ØØ         LDA #$00
CØ59 85 FB         STA $FB
CØ5B A9 60         LDA #$60
CØ5D 85 FC         STA $FC
CØ5F AØ ØØ         LDY #$00
CØ61 A9 ØØ         LDA #$00
CØ63 91 FB         STA ($FB),Y
CØ65 C8            INY
CØ66 DØ FB         BNE $C063
CØ68 E6 FC         INC $FC
CØ6A A6 FC         LDX $FC
CØ6C EØ 80         CPX #$80
CØ6E DØ F3         BNE $C063
CØ70 AD 85 CØ      LDA $C085
CØ73 A2 ØØ         LDX #$00
CØ75 9D ØØ 40      STA $4000,X
CØ78 9D ØØ 41      STA $4100,X
CØ7B 9D ØØ 42      STA $4200,X
CØ7E 9D ØØ 43      STA $4300,X
CØ81 E8            INX
CØ82 DØ F1         BNE $C075
CØ84 60            RTS
```

21. Plot

This routine plots a point on the high res screen . It requires two parameters: the X coordinate (0-319) and the Y coordinate (0-199) to be plotted.

The syntax is SYS 49286,X coord, Y coord.

```
PAL (C)1979 BRAD TEMPLETON
2
20:     CØ8A                            .OPT P,OO
30:     CØ8A                        *=      $CØ8A
40:     CØ8A            XCOORD      =       $14


;AND $15
50:     CØ8A            TEMP        =       $FD
60:     CØ8A            SCREEN      =       $6ØØØ
70:     CØ8A            CHECKCOM    =       $AEFD
80:     CØ8A            COORD       =       $B7EB
90:     CØ8A            FALSE       =       255
100:    CØ8A            TRUE        =       Ø
130:    CØ8A A9 ØØ      SET         LDA     #TRUE
140:    CØ8C 8D 3A C1   SET1        STA     RSFLAG

150:    CØ8F 20 FD AE               JSR     CHECKC
OM
160:    CØ92 2Ø EB B7               JSR     COORD
170:    CØ95 EØ C8                  CPX     #200
180:    CØ97 BØ 5E                  BCS     TOOBIG

190:    CØ99 A5 14                  LDA     XCOORD

200:    CØ9B C9 4Ø                  CMP     #<32Ø
210:    CØ9D A5 15                  LDA     XCOORD
+1
```

```
220:    CØ9F E9 Ø1          SBC   #>320
230:    CØA1 BØ 54          BCS   TOOBIG

240:    CØA3 8A             TXA
250:    CØA4 4A             LSR
260:    CØA5 4A             LSR
270:    CØA6 4A             LSR
280:    CØA7 ØA             ASL
290:    CØA8 A8             TAY
300:    CØA9 B9 F8 CØ       LDA   TABLE,
Y       ;MULTIPLY PUT IN
310:    CØAC 85 FD          STA   TEMP
320:    CØAE B9 F9 CØ       LDA   TABLE+
1,Y
330:    CØB1 85 FE          STA   TEMP+1

340:    CØB3 8A             TXA
350:    CØB4 29 Ø7          AND   #%0000
Ø111
360:    CØB6 18             CLC
370:    CØB7 65 FD          ADC   TEMP
380:    CØB9 85 FD          STA   TEMP
390:    CØBB A5 FE          LDA   TEMP+1

400:    CØBD 69 ØØ          ADC   #Ø
410:    CØBF 85 FE          STA   TEMP+1

420:    CØC1 A5 14          LDA   XCOORD

430:    CØC3 29 Ø7          AND   #%0000
Ø111
440:    CØC5 A8             TAY
450:    CØC6 A5 14          LDA   XCOORD

460:    CØC8 29 F8          AND   #%1111
1ØØØ
470:    CØCA 18             CLC
480:    CØCB 65 FD          ADC   TEMP
490:    CØCD 85 FD          STA   TEMP
500:    CØCF A5 FE          LDA   TEMP+1
```

```
510:     CØD1 65 15              ADC    XCOORD
+1
520:     CØD3 85 FE              STA    TEMP+1

530:     CØD5 A5 FD              LDA    TEMP
540:     CØD7 18                 CLC
550:     CØD8 69 ØØ              ADC    #<SCRE
EN
560:     CØDA 85 FD              STA    TEMP
570:     CØDC A5 FE              LDA    TEMP+1

580:     CØDE 69 6Ø              ADC    #>SCRE
EN
590:     CØEØ 85 FE              STA    TEMP+1

600:     CØE2 A2 ØØ              LDX    #Ø
610:     CØE4 A1 FD              LDA    (TEMP,
X)
620:     CØE6 2C 3A C1           BIT    RSFLAG

630:     CØE9 10 Ø6              BPL    SET2
640:     CØEB 39 32 C1           AND    ANDMAS
K,Y
650:     CØEE 4C F4 CØ           JMP    SET3
660:     CØF1 19 2A C1 SET2      ORA    ORMASK
,Y
670:     CØF4 81 FD    SET3      STA    (TEMP,
X)
680:     CØF6 60                 RTS
690:     CØF7 60       TOOBIG    RTS
700:     CØF8          N         =      32Ø
710:     CØF8 ØØ ØØ 4Ø TABLE     .WORDØ*N,1*
N,2*N,3*N,4*N
720:     C1Ø2 4Ø Ø6 8Ø           .WORD5*N,6*
N,7*N,8*N,9*N
730:     C1ØC 8Ø ØC CØ           .WORD1Ø*N,1
1*N,12*N,13*N,14*N
740:     C116 CØ 12 ØØ           .WORD15*N,1
6*N,17*N,18*N,19*N
750:     C12Ø ØØ 19 4Ø           .WORD2Ø*N,2
1*N,22*N,23*N,24*N
```

```
                              ;
770:    C12A 80       ORMASK      .BYT %10000
000
780:    C12B 40                   .BYT %01000
000
790:    C12C 20                   .BYT %00100
000
800:    C12D 10                   .BYT %00010
000
810:    C12E 08                   .BYT %00001
000
820:    C12F 04                   .BYT %00000
100
830:    C130 02                   .BYT %00000
010
840:    C131 01                   .BYT %00000
001
                              ;
860:    C132 7F       ANDMASK     .BYT %01111
111
870:    C133 BF                   .BYT %10111
111
880:    C134 DF                   .BYT %11011
111
890:    C135 EF                   .BYT %11101
111
900:    C136 F7                   .BYT %11110
111
910:    C137 FB                   .BYT %11111
011
920:    C138 FD                   .BYT %11111
101
930:    C139 FE                   .BYT %11111
110
                              ;
950:    C13A 00       RSFLAG      .BYT 0
]C08A-C13B

READY.
```

B*
```
    PC  SR AC XR YR SP
.;97FE 72 00 00 01 F6
.
C08A A9 00          LDA #$00
C08C 8D 3A C1       STA $C13A
C08F 20 FD AE       JSR $AEFD
C092 20 EB B7       JSR $B7EB
C095 E0 C8          CPX #$C8
C097 B0 5E          BCS $C0F7
C099 A5 14          LDA $14
C09B C9 40          CMP #$40
C09D A5 15          LDA $15
C09F E9 01          SBC #$01
C0A1 B0 54          BCS $C0F7
C0A3 8A             TXA
C0A4 4A             LSR
C0A5 4A             LSR
C0A6 4A             LSR
C0A7 0A             ASL
C0A8 A8             TAY
C0A9 B9 F8 C0       LDA $C0F8,Y
C0AC 85 FD          STA $FD
C0AE B9 F9 C0       LDA $C0F9,Y
C0B1 85 FE          STA $FE
C0B3 8A             TXA
C0B4 29 07          AND #$07
C0B6 18             CLC
C0B7 65 FD          ADC $FD
C0B9 85 FD          STA $FD
C0BB A5 FE          LDA $FE
C0BD 69 00          ADC #$00
C0BF 85 FE          STA $FE
C0C1 A5 14          LDA $14
C0C3 29 07          AND #$07
C0C5 A8             TAY
C0C6 A5 14          LDA $14
C0C8 29 F8          AND #$F8
C0CA 18             CLC
C0CB 65 FD          ADC $FD
C0CD 85 FD          STA $FD
```

```
CØCF A5 FE        LDA $FE
CØD1 65 15        ADC $15
CØD3 85 FE        STA $FE
CØD5 A5 FD        LDA $FD
CØD7 18           CLC
CØD8 69 ØØ        ADC #$ØØ
CØDA 85 FD        STA $FD
CØDC A5 FE        LDA $FE
CØDE 69 6Ø        ADC #$6Ø
CØEØ 85 FE        STA $FE
CØE2 A2 ØØ        LDX #$ØØ
CØE4 A1 FD        LDA ($FD,X)
CØE6 2C 3A C1     BIT $C13A
CØE9 1Ø Ø6        BPL $CØF1
CØEB 39 32 C1     AND $C132,Y
CØEE 4C F4 CØ     JMP $CØF4
CØF1 19 2A C1     ORA $C12A,Y
CØF4 81 FD        STA ($FD,X)
CØF6 6Ø           RTS
CØF7 6Ø           RTS
   .
   .
   .
   .
.:CØF8 ØØ ØØ 4Ø Ø1 8Ø Ø2 CØ Ø3
.:C1ØØ ØØ Ø5 4Ø Ø6 8Ø Ø7 CØ Ø8
.:C1Ø8 ØØ ØA 4Ø ØB 8Ø ØC CØ ØD
.:C11Ø ØØ ØF 4Ø 1Ø 8Ø 11 CØ 12
.:C118 ØØ 14 4Ø 15 8Ø 16 CØ 17
.:C12Ø ØØ 19 4Ø 1A 8Ø 1B CØ 1C
.:C128 ØØ 1E 8Ø 4Ø 2Ø 1Ø Ø8 Ø4
.:C13Ø Ø2 Ø1 7F BF DF EF F7 FB
.:C138 FD FE ØØ C2 C9 FØ Ø8 2Ø
   .
```

22. Unplot

This routine is complementary to Plot. It unplots a point on the high res screen. Just type in the routine below and unplot is ready.

To use type SYS 49286,X,Y

```
30 *=$C086
40 LDA #$FF
50 BNE SET1
```

READY.

```
B*
    PC   SR AC XR YR SP
.}97FE 72 00 00 01 F6
•
C086 A9 FF        LDA #$FF
C088 D0 02        BNE $C08C
•
```

23. Char

This routine puts a character onto the high res screen. You specify three parameters: the X coordinate (0-39), the Y coordinate (0-24) and the character code (screen code).

The syntax is SYS 49467,X,Y,char code

```
PAL (C)1979 BRAD TEMPLETON
2
20:     C13B                        .OPT P,OO
30:     C13B                        *=    $C13B
                              ;
                              ;CHAR X,Y,CHARACTER,
                              ;EOR OR DELETE
70:     C13B 4C 48 B2  ERROR        JMP   $B248
80:     C13E 20 FD AE               JSR   $AEFD
90:     C141 20 1D C2               JSR   PARAMS
100:    C144 A5 14                  LDA   $14
100:    C146 C9 28                  CMP   #40
100:    C148 B0 F1                  BCS   ERROR
110:    C14A 8D 4B C2               STA   XSTORE
120:    C14D 20 FD AE               JSR   $AEFD
130:    C150 20 1D C2               JSR   PARAMS
140:    C153 A5 14                  LDA   $14
140:    C155 C9 19                  CMP   #25
140:    C157 B0 E2                  BCS   ERROR
150:    C159 8D 4C C2               STA   YSTORE
                              ;TOTAL = Y*320 + X*8
170:    C15C AD 4B C2               LDA   XSTORE
180:    C15F 8D 48 C2               STA   MULT1
190:    C162 A9 08                  LDA   #8
200:    C164 8D 49 C2               STA   MULT2
210:    C167 20 2B C2               JSR   MULTIPLY
220:    C16A AD 46 C2               LDA   RESULT
```

```
230:    C16D 85 FB                      STA     *FB
240:    C16F AD 47 C2                   LDA     RESULT+1
250:    C172 85 FC                      STA     *FC
                                ;
                                ;NOW Y=320*Y
280:    C174 AD 4C C2                   LDA     YSTORE
290:    C177 8D 48 C2                   STA     MULT1
300:    C17A A9 28                      LDA     #40
310:    C17C 8D 49 C2                   STA     MULT2
320:    C17F 20 2B C2                   JSR     MULTIPLY
330:    C182 AD 46 C2                   LDA     RESULT
330:    C185 8D 50 C2                   STA     STORERES
330:    C188 AD 47 C2                   LDA     RESULT+1
330:    C18B 8D 51 C2                   STA     STORERES+1
340:    C18E A2 07                      LDX     #7
350:    C190 AD 46 C2 LOOP12            LDA     RESULT
350:    C193 6D 50 C2                   ADC     STORERES
360:    C196 8D 46 C2                   STA     RESULT
360:    C199 AD 47 C2                   LDA     RESULT+1
370:    C19C 69 00                      ADC     #0
370:    C19E 8D 47 C2                   STA     RESULT+1
380:    C1A1 CA                         DEX
390:    C1A2 D0 EC                      BNE     LOOP12
400:    C1A4 A2 07                      LDX     #7
410:    C1A6 AD 47 C2 LOOP14            LDA     RESULT+1
420:    C1A9 18                         CLC
420:    C1AA 6D 51 C2                   ADC     STORERES+1
430:    C1AD 8D 47 C2                   STA     RESULT+1
440:    C1B0 CA                         DEX
450:    C1B1 D0 F3                      BNE     LOOP14
460:    C1B3 AD 47 C2                   LDA     RESULT+1
470:    C1B6 18                         CLC
470:    C1B7 69 60                      ADC     #$60
480:    C1B9 8D 47 C2                   STA     RESULT+1
490:    C1BC A5 FB                      LDA     *FB
500:    C1BE 18                         CLC
500:    C1BF 6D 46 C2                   ADC     RESULT
510:    C1C2 85 FB                      STA     *FB
520:    C1C4 A5 FC                      LDA     *FC
530:    C1C6 6D 47 C2                   ADC     RESULT+1
540:    C1C9 85 FC                      STA     *FC
```

```
550:    C1CB 20 FD AE            JSR   $AEFD
560:    C1CE 20 1D C2            JSR   PARAMS
570:    C1D1 A5 14               LDA   $14
580:    C1D3 8D 4E C2            STA   CHAR
590:    C1D6 AD 4E C2            LDA   CHAR
600:    C1D9 8D 48 C2            STA   MULT1
610:    C1DC A9 08               LDA   #8
620:    C1DE 8D 49 C2            STA   MULT2
630:    C1E1 20 2B C2            JSR   MULTIPLY
640:    C1E4 AD 46 C2            LDA   RESULT
                            ;CHARACTER LOCATION
650:    C1E7 85 FD               STA   $FD
660:    C1E9 AD 47 C2            LDA   RESULT+1
670:    C1EC 18                  CLC
                            ;ADD $D0 TO $D000
670:    C1ED 69 D0               ADC   #$D0
680:    C1EF 85 FE               STA   $FE
690:    C1F1 A9 00               LDA   #0
690:    C1F3 8D 4A C2            STA   COUNT
690:    C1F6 78                  SEI
690:    C1F7 A9 33               LDA   #51
690:    C1F9 85 01               STA   $01
700:    C1FB A0 00               LDY   #0
710:    C1FD B1 FD      LOOP1    LDA   ($FD),Y
720:    C1FF 91 FB               STA   ($FB),Y
730:    C201 E6 FB               INC   $FB
730:    C203 D0 02               BNE   N1
740:    C205 E6 FC               INC   $FC
750:    C207 E6 FD      N1       INC   $FD
760:    C209 D0 02               BNE   N2
770:    C20B E6 FE               INC   $FE
780:    C20D EE 4A C2 N2         INC   COUNT
790:    C210 AD 4A C2            LDA   COUNT
800:    C213 C9 08               CMP   #8
810:    C215 D0 E6               BNE   LOOP1
820:    C217 A9 37               LDA   #55
820:    C219 85 01               STA   1
820:    C21B 58                  CLI
820:    C21C 60                  RTS
830:    C21D 20 8A AD PARAMS     JSR   $AD8A
840:    C220 20 F7 B7            JSR   $B7F7
```

```
850:    C223 A5 15              LDA   #15
850:    C225 F0 03              BEQ   FINROUT
860:    C227 4C 48 B2           JMP   $B248
860:    C22A 60        FINROUT  RTS
870:    C22B A9 00     MULTIPLY LDA   #0
880:    C22D 8D 46 C2           STA   RESULT
890:    C230 A2 08              LDX   #8
900:    C232 4E 48 C2 LOOP21    LSR   MULT1
910:    C235 90 04              BCC   LOOP9
920:    C237 18                 CLC
930:    C238 6D 49 C2           ADC   MULT2
940:    C23B 6A       LOOP9     ROR   A
950:    C23C 6E 46 C2           ROR   RESULT
960:    C23F CA                 DEX
970:    C240 D0 F0              BNE   LOOP21
980:    C242 8D 47 C2           STA   RESULT+1
990:    C245 60                 RTS
1000:   C246 00 00     RESULT   .WORD0
1010:   C248 00        MULT1    .BYT 0
1020:   C249 00        MULT2    .BYT 0
1030:   C24A 00        COUNT    .BYT 0
1040:   C24B 00        XSTORE   .BYT 0
1050:   C24C 00        YSTORE   .BYT 0
1060:   C24D 00        EORFLAG  .BYT 0
1070:   C24E 00        CHAR     .BYT 0
1080:   C24F 00        STORE    .BYT 0
1090:   C250 00 00     STORERES .WORD0
JC13B-C252
```

READY.

```
        B*
          PC  SR AC XR YR SP
        .;97FE 72 00 00 01 F6
        .
        C13B 4C 48 B2      JMP  $B248
        C13E 20 FD AE      JSR  $AEFD
        C141 20 1D C2      JSR  $C21D
```

```
C144 A5 14        LDA $14
C146 C9 28        CMP #$28
C148 B0 F1        BCS $C13B
C14A 8D 4B C2     STA $C24B
C14D 20 FD AE     JSR $AEFD
C150 20 1D C2     JSR $C21D
C153 A5 14        LDA $14
C155 C9 19        CMP #$19
C157 B0 E2        BCS $C13B
C159 8D 4C C2     STA $C24C
C15C AD 4B C2     LDA $C24B
C15F 8D 48 C2     STA $C248
C162 A9 08        LDA #$08
C164 8D 49 C2     STA $C249
C167 20 2B C2     JSR $C22B
C16A AD 46 C2     LDA $C246
C16D 85 FB        STA $FB
C16F AD 47 C2     LDA $C247
C172 85 FC        STA $FC
C174 AD 4C C2     LDA $C24C
C177 8D 48 C2     STA $C248
C17A A9 28        LDA #$28
C17C 8D 49 C2     STA $C249
C17F 20 2B C2     JSR $C22B
C182 AD 46 C2     LDA $C246
C185 8D 50 C2     STA $C250
C188 AD 47 C2     LDA $C247
C18B 8D 51 C2     STA $C251
C18E A2 07        LDX #$07
C190 AD 46 C2     LDA $C246
C193 6D 50 C2     ADC $C250
C196 8D 46 C2     STA $C246
C199 AD 47 C2     LDA $C247
C19C 69 00        ADC #$00
C19E 8D 47 C2     STA $C247
C1A1 CA           DEX
C1A2 D0 EC        BNE $C190
C1A4 A2 07        LDX #$07
C1A6 AD 47 C2     LDA $C247
C1A9 18           CLC
C1AA 6D 51 C2     ADC $C251
```

```
C1AD 8D 47 C2        STA $C247
C1B0 CA              DEX
C1B1 D0 F3           BNE $C1A6
C1B3 AD 47 C2        LDA $C247
C1B6 18              CLC
C1B7 69 60           ADC #$60
C1B9 8D 47 C2        STA $C247
C1BC A5 FB           LDA $FB
C1BE 18              CLC
C1BF 6D 46 C2        ADC $C246
C1C2 85 FB           STA $FB
C1C4 A5 FC           LDA $FC
C1C6 6D 47 C2        ADC $C247
C1C9 85 FC           STA $FC
C1CB 20 FD AE        JSR $AEFD
C1CE 20 1D C2        JSR $C21D
C1D1 A5 14           LDA $14
C1D3 8D 4E C2        STA $C24E
C1D6 AD 4E C2        LDA $C24E
C1D9 8D 48 C2        STA $C248
C1DC A9 08           LDA #$08
C1DE 8D 49 C2        STA $C249
C1E1 20 2B C2        JSR $C22B
C1E4 AD 46 C2        LDA $C246
C1E7 85 FD           STA $FD
C1E9 AD 47 C2        LDA $C247
C1EC 18              CLC
C1ED 69 D0           ADC #$D0
C1EF 85 FE           STA $FE
C1F1 A9 00           LDA #$00
C1F3 8D 4A C2        STA $C24A
C1F6 78              SEI
C1F7 A9 33           LDA #$33
C1F9 85 01           STA $01
C1FB A0 00           LDY #$00
C1FD B1 FD           LDA ($FD),Y
C1FF 91 FB           STA ($FB),Y
C201 E6 FB           INC $FB
C203 D0 02           BNE $C207
C205 E6 FC           INC $FC
C207 E6 FD           INC $FD
```

```
C209 DØ Ø2        BNE $C2ØD
C2ØB E6 FE        INC $FE
C2ØD EE 4A C2     INC $C24A
C21Ø AD 4A C2     LDA $C24A
C213 C9 Ø8        CMP #$Ø8
C215 DØ E6        BNE $C1FD
C217 A9 37        LDA #$37
C219 85 Ø1        STA $Ø1
C21B 58           CLI
C21C 6Ø           RTS
C21D 2Ø 8A AD     JSR $AD8A
C22Ø 2Ø F7 B7     JSR $B7F7
C223 A5 15        LDA $15
C225 FØ Ø3        BEQ $C22A
C227 4C 48 B2     JMP $B248
C22A 6Ø           RTS
C22B A9 ØØ        LDA #$ØØ
C22D 8D 46 C2     STA $C246
C23Ø A2 Ø8        LDX #$Ø8
C232 4E 48 C2     LSR $C248
C235 9Ø Ø4        BCC $C23B
C237 18           CLC
C238 6D 49 C2     ADC $C249
C23B 6A           ROR
C23C 6E 46 C2     ROR $C246
C23F CA           DEX
C24Ø DØ FØ        BNE $C232
C242 8D 47 C2     STA $C247
C245 6Ø           RTS
  .
  .
  .
  .
.:C246 ØØ ØØ ØØ ØØ ØØ ØØ ØØ ØØ
.:C24E ØØ ØØ ØØ ØØ 1Ø CF A5 BA
```

97

24. Change bank

This routine allows easy access to the four 16K banks accessible by the VIC II chip. It does not copy the character set down. To do this, use the copy routine given above.

The syntax is SYS 828, bank (0-3)

where bank 0 is 0-16383 , 1 is 16384 to 32767 and so on.

```
PAL  (C)1979  BRAD  TEMPLETON
2
20:       033C                              .OPT  P,OO
30:       033C                              *=    828
                                     ;
                                     ;ROUTINE  TO  CHANGE
                                     ;BANK  FOR
                                     ;VIC  II  CHIP
                                     ;
                                     ;SYNTAX
                                     ;
                                     ;SYS  828,BANK  (0-3)
                                     ;
130:      033C  20  FD  AE            JSR    $AEFD
140:      033F  20  9E  B7            JSR    $B79E
150:      0342  8A                    TXA
160:      0343  C9  05                CMP    #5
170:      0345  90  03                BCC    MORE
180:      0347  4C  48  B2            JMP    $B248
                                     ;
200:      034A  AA           MORE     TAX
210:      034B  BD  63  03            LDA    L53272,X
220:      034E  8D  18  DO            STA    53272
230:      0351  BD  67  03            LDA    L648,X
240:      0354  8D  88  02            STA    648
```

```
250:     0357 BD 6B 03              LDA  L56576,X
260:     035A 8D 00 DD              STA  56576
270:     035D A9 93                 LDA  #"♣
280:     035F 20 D2 FF              JSR  $FFD2
290:     0362 60                    RTS
                          ;
310:     0363 15 15 15 L53272  .BYT 21,21,21,21
320:     0367 04 04 04 L648    .BYT 4,4,4,4
330:     036B 47 46 45 L56576  .BYT 71,70,69,68
]033C-036F

READY.


         B*
            PC  SR AC XR YR SP
         .¦97FE 72 00 00 01 F6
         .
         033C 20 FD AE      JSR $AEFD
         033F 20 9E B7      JSR $B79E
         0342 8A            TXA
         0343 C9 05         CMP #$05
         0345 90 03         BCC $034A
         0347 4C 48 B2      JMP $B248
         034A AA            TAX
         034B BD 63 03      LDA $0363,X
         034E 8D 18 D0      STA $D018
         0351 BD 67 03      LDA $0367,X
         0354 8D 88 02      STA $0288
         0357 BD 6B 03      LDA $036B,X
         035A 8D 00 DD      STA $DD00
         035D A9 93         LDA #$93
         035F 20 D2 FF      JSR $FFD2
         0362 60            RTS
         .
         .
         .
         .
         .:0363 15 15 15 15 04 04 04 04
         .:036B 47 46 45 44 0D 20 74 03
         .
```

99

25. Invert

This routine inverts all or some of the high res screen (it can invert any part of memory).

The syntax is SYS 49746,start,invert

```
PAL (C)1979 BRAD TEMPLETON
2
20:     C252                            .OPT P,OO
30:     C252                            *=    $C252
                                  ;FILL ROUTINE
                                  ;
                                  ;USES $FB AND $FC
                                  ;STORE TOP ADDRESS
                                  ;IN 828 AND 829
                                  ;SCAN PAST COMMA
90:     C252 20 FD AE             JSR   $AEFD
                                  ;READ 16 BIT NUMBER
100:    C255 20 8A AD             JSR   $AD8A
                                  ;PUT INTO $14 AND $15
110:    C258 20 F7 B7             JSR   $B7F7
120:    C25B A5 14                LDA   $14
120:    C25D 85 FB                STA   $FB
130:    C25F A5 15                LDA   $15
130:    C261 85 FC                STA   $FC
                                  ;
150:    C263 20 FD AE             JSR   $AEFD
                                  ;SCAN PAST NEXT COMMA
160:    C266 20 8A AD             JSR   $AD8A
170:    C269 20 F7 B7             JSR   $B7F7
180:    C26C A5 14                LDA   $14
180:    C26E 8D 3C 03             STA   828
190:    C271 A5 15                LDA   $15
190:    C273 8D 3D 03             STA   829
```

```
210:    C276 A0 00      LOOP       LDY  #0
220:    C278 A9 FF                  LDA  #255
230:    C27A 51 FB                  EOR  (#FB),Y
240:    C27C 91 FB                  STA  (#FB),Y
250:    C27E 20 95 C2              JSR  ADD
260:    C281 A5 FB                  LDA  #FB
260:    C283 CD 3C 03              CMP  828
260:    C286 F0 03                  BEQ  CHECK
270:    C288 4C 76 C2              JMP  LOOP
280:    C28B A5 FC      CHECK      LDA  #FC
280:    C28D CD 3D 03              CMP  829
280:    C290 F0 0B                  BEQ  FINISH
290:    C292 4C 76 C2              JMP  LOOP
300:    C295 E6 FB      ADD        INC  #FB
300:    C297 F0 01                  BEQ  FCPLUS1
310:    C299 60                     RTS
320:    C29A E6 FC      FCPLUS1    INC  #FC
320:    C29C 60                     RTS
330:    C29D 60         FINISH     RTS
]C252-C29E
```

READY.

```
B*
     PC   SR AC XR YR SP
.197FE 72 00 00 01 F6
.
C252 20 FD AE      JSR  #AEFD
C255 20 8A AD      JSR  #AD8A
C258 20 F7 B7      JSR  #B7F7
C25B A5 14         LDA  #14
C25D 85 FB         STA  #FB
C25F A5 15         LDA  #15
C261 85 FC         STA  #FC
C263 20 FD AE      JSR  #AEFD
```

```
C266 20 8A AD      JSR $AD8A
C269 20 F7 B7      JSR $B7F7
C26C A5 14         LDA $14
C26E 8D 3C 03      STA $033C
C271 A5 15         LDA $15
C273 8D 3D 03      STA $033D
C276 A0 00         LDY #$00
C278 A9 FF         LDA #$FF
C27A 51 FB         EOR ($FB),Y
C27C 91 FB         STA ($FB),Y
C27E 20 95 C2      JSR $C295
C281 A5 FB         LDA $FB
C283 CD 3C 03      CMP $033C
C286 F0 03         BEQ $C28B
C288 4C 76 C2      JMP $C276
C28B A5 FC         LDA $FC
C28D CD 3D 03      CMP $033D
C290 F0 0B         BEQ $C29D
C292 4C 76 C2      JMP $C276
C295 E6 FB         INC $FB
C297 F0 01         BEQ $C29A
C299 60            RTS
C29A E6 FC         INC $FC
C29C 60            RTS
C29D 60            RTS
```

26. Organ

The following is a simple interrupt driven organ program. It allows you to play a tune on the keyboard whether a program is running or not. The program could run with a sound shaping program, for example.

The keys used are as follows:

q w e r t y u i o p @ * !
and the space bar to turn the notes off

To turn on the organ type SYS 49152.

```
PAL  (C) 1979  BRAD  TEMPLETON
2
20:    C000                          .OPT P,OO
30:    C000                          *=    $C000
                          ;
50:    C000 78                       SEI
50:    C001 A9 1F                    LDA   #<MAIN

50:    C003 8D 14 03                 STA   788
60:    C006 A9 C0                    LDA   #>MAIN

60:    C008 8D 15 03                 STA   789
70:    C00B A9 0F                    LDA   #15
70:    C00D 8D 18 D4                 STA   54296
70:    C010 A9 21                    LDA   #33
70:    C012 8D 04 D4                 STA   54276
70:    C015 A9 38                    LDA   #<56
70:    C017 8D 05 D4                 STA   54277
70:    C01A 8D 06 D4                 STA   54278
70:    C01D 58                       CLI
70:    C01E 60                       RTS
```

103

```
90:      CØ1F A5 C5      MAIN        LDA   197
100:     CØ21 A2 ØØ                  LDX   #Ø
100:     CØ23 AØ ØØ                  LDY   #Ø
110:     CØ25 DD 43 CØ LOOP          CMP   KEYDAT
A,X
120:     CØ28 FØ ØA                  BEQ   PLAYNO
TE
130:     CØ2A E8                     INX
130:     CØ2B C8                     INY
130:     CØ2C C8                     INY
140:     CØ2D EØ ØF                  CPX   #15
150:     CØ2F DØ F4                  BNE   LOOP
160:     CØ31 4C 31 EA               JMP   $EA31
                         ;
180:     CØ34                PLAYNOTE =     *
190:     CØ34 B9 51 CØ               LDA   NOTETA
BLE,Y
190:     CØ37 8D Ø1 D4               STA   54273
190:     CØ3A B9 52 CØ               LDA   NOTETA
BLE+1,Y
190:     CØ3D 8D ØØ D4               STA   54272
200:     CØ40 4C 31 EA               JMP   $EA31
210:     CØ43 3E Ø9 ØE KEYDATA .BYT 62,9,1
4,17,22,25,3Ø,33,38,41
220:     CØ4D 2E 31 36           .BYT 46,49,
54,6Ø
                         ;
240:     CØ51 11 25 13 NOTETABLE.BYT 17,37,
19,63,21,154,22,227
250:     CØ59 19 B1 1C           .BYT 25,177
,28,214,32,94,34,75,38,126,43,52
260:     CØ65 2D C6 33           .BYT 45,198
,51,97,57,172,Ø,Ø
]CØØØ-CØ6D
```

B*

```
     PC   SR AC XR YR SP
.]97FE 72 ØØ ØØ Ø1 F6
```

```
C000 78              SEI
C001 A9 1F           LDA #$1F
C003 8D 14 03        STA $0314
C006 A9 C0           LDA #$C0
C008 8D 15 03        STA $0315
C00B A9 0F           LDA #$0F
C00D 8D 18 D4        STA $D418
C010 A9 21           LDA #$21
C012 8D 04 D4        STA $D404
C015 A9 38           LDA #$38
C017 8D 05 D4        STA $D405
C01A 8D 06 D4        STA $D406
C01D 58              CLI
C01E 60              RTS
C01F A5 C5           LDA $C5
C021 A2 00           LDX #$00
C023 A0 00           LDY #$00
C025 DD 43 C0        CMP $C043,X
C028 F0 0A           BEQ $C034
C02A E8              INX
C02B C8              INY
C02C C8              INY
C02D E0 0F           CPX #$0F
C02F D0 F4           BNE $C025
C031 4C 31 EA        JMP $EA31
C034 B9 51 C0        LDA $C051,Y
C037 8D 01 D4        STA $D401
C03A B9 52 C0        LDA $C052,Y
C03D 8D 00 D4        STA $D400
C040 4C 31 EA        JMP $EA31
     .
     .
.:C043 3E 09 0E 11 16 19 1E 21
.:C04B 26 29 2E 31 36 3C 11 25
.:C053 13 3F 15 9A 16 E3 19 B1
.:C05B 1C D6 20 5E 22 4B 26 7E
.:C063 2B 34 2D C6 33 61 39 AC
.:C06B 00 00 80 D0 F3 AD 85 C0
```

27. Sound

This routine makes sound much easier to use. It allows you to set the voice, volume, frequency and waveform for the sound.

The syntax is SYS 16384,voice,volume,frequency,waveform.

The voice is between 1 and 3. The volume is between 0 and 15. The frequency is between 0 and 65535. The waveform is one of 17 (triangle), 33 (sawtooth) and 129 (noise). Pulse waveform is not implemented. It can be set but it will not function.

The ADSR and all other features of the SID chip are set automatically.

To produce a rising tone the following routine could be used.

```
FOR A = 0 TO 65535 STEP100 :
SYS16384,1,15,A,33:NEXT:SYS16384,1,0,0,33
```

The last statement turns off the sound.

```
PAL (C)1979 BRAD TEMPLETON
2
20:     4000                        .OPT P,00
30:     4000                        *=    $4000
                            ;
                            ; SOUND ROUTINE
                            ;
                            ;SYNTAX ;
                            ;
                            ; SYS 16384,VOICE,
                            ; VOLUME,FREQ,WAVE
110:    4000 20 FD AE                JSR   $AEFD
120:    4003 20 8A AD                JSR   $AD8A
```

```
130:    4006 20 F7 B7          JSR    $B7F7
140:    4009 A5 15             LDA    $15
150:    400B D0 3F             BNE    IQERR
160:    400D A5 14             LDA    $14
170:    400F 8D DA 40          STA    VOICE
                          ;
190:    4012 20 FD AE          JSR    $AEFD
200:    4015 20 8A AD          JSR    $AD8A
210:    4018 20 F7 B7          JSR    $B7F7
220:    401B A5 15             LDA    $15
230:    401D D0 2D             BNE    IQERR
240:    401F A5 14             LDA    $14
250:    4021 8D DB 40          STA    VOLUME
                          ;
270:    4024 20 FD AE          JSR    $AEFD
280:    4027 20 8A AD          JSR    $AD8A
290:    402A 20 F7 B7          JSR    $B7F7
300:    402D A5 14             LDA    $14
310:    402F 8D DD 40          STA    FREQ
320:    4032 A5 15             LDA    $15
330:    4034 8D DE 40          STA    FREQ+1
                          ;
350:    4037 20 FD AE          JSR    $AEFD
360:    403A 20 8A AD          JSR    $AD8A
370:    403D 20 F7 B7          JSR    $B7F7
380:    4040 A5 15             LDA    $15
390:    4042 D0 08             BNE    IQERR
400:    4044 A5 14             LDA    $14
410:    4046 8D DC 40          STA    WAVE
420:    4049 4C 4F 40          JMP    DO
430:    404C 4C 48 B2 IQERR    JMP    $B248
                          ;
450:    404F A2 00    DO       LDX    #0
450:    4051 AD DC 40          LDA    WAVE
460:    4054 DD DF 40 LOP      CMP    WAVETABLE,X
470:    4057 F0 08             BEQ    MORE
480:    4059 E8               INX
480:    405A E0 04             CPX    #4
490:    405C D0 F6             BNE    LOP
500:    405E 4C 4C 40          JMP    IQERR
510:    4061 AD DA 40 MORE     LDA    VOICE
```

```
520:    4064 F0 E6              BEQ   IQERR
530:    4066 C9 04              CMP   #4
540:    4068 B0 E2              BCS   IQERR
                            ;
560:    406A AD DB 40          LDA   VOLUME
570:    406D C9 10              CMP   #16
580:    406F B0 DB              BCS   IQERR
                            ;
600:    4071 AD DB 40          LDA   VOLUME
610:    4074 8D 18 D4          STA   54296
                            ;
630:    4077 AD DA 40          LDA   VOICE
                            ;
650:    407A C9 01              CMP   #1
660:    407C F0 07              BEQ   VOICE1
670:    407E C9 02              CMP   #2
680:    4080 F0 20              BEQ   VOICE2
690:    4082 4C BF 40          JMP   VOICE3
                            ;
710:    4085 AD DC 40  VOICE1  LDA   WAVE
720:    4088 8D 04 D4          STA   54276
730:    408B A9 80              LDA   #128
740:    408D 8D 05 D4          STA   54277
750:    4090 8D 06 D4          STA   54278
760:    4093 AD DD 40          LDA   FREQ
770:    4096 8D 00 D4          STA   54272
780:    4099 AD DE 40          LDA   FREQ+1
790:    409C 8D 01 D4          STA   54273
800:    409F 4C D9 40          JMP   FINISH
                            ;
820:    40A2 AD DC 40  VOICE2  LDA   WAVE
830:    40A5 8D 0B D4          STA   54283
840:    40A8 A9 80              LDA   #128
850:    40AA 8D 0C D4          STA   54284
860:    40AD 8D 0D D4          STA   54285
870:    40B0 AD DD 40          LDA   FREQ
880:    40B3 8D 07 D4          STA   54279
890:    40B6 AD DE 40          LDA   FREQ+1
900:    40B9 8D 08 D4          STA   54280
910:    40BC 4C D9 40          JMP   FINISH
                            ;
```

```
930:    40BF AD DC 40 VOICE3    LDA   WAVE
940:    40C2 8D 12 D4           STA   54290
950:    40C5 A9 80             LDA   #128
960:    40C7 8D 13 D4           STA   54291
970:    40CA 8D 14 D4           STA   54292
980:    40CD AD DD 40           LDA   FREQ
990:    40D0 8D 0E D4           STA   54286
1000:   40D3 AD DE 40           LDA   FREQ+1
1010:   40D6 8D 0F D4           STA   54287
                               ;
1030:   40D9 60      FINISH    RTS
1040:   40DA 00      VOICE     .BYT 0
1050:   40DB 00      VOLUME    .BYT 0
1060:   40DC 00      WAVE      .BYT 0
1070:   40DD 00 00   FREQ      .WORD0
1080:   40DF 11 21 41 WAVETABLE.BYT 17,33,65,129
J4000-40E3
```

READY.


```
        B*
          PC   SR AC XR YR SP
        .J97FE 72 00 00 01 F6
        .
        4000 20 FD AE       JSR  $AEFD
        4003 20 8A AD       JSR  $AD8A
        4006 20 F7 B7       JSR  $B7F7
        4009 A5 15          LDA  $15
        400B D0 3F          BNE  $404C
        400D A5 14          LDA  $14
        400F 8D DA 40       STA  $40DA
        4012 20 FD AE       JSR  $AEFD
        4015 20 8A AD       JSR  $AD8A
        4018 20 F7 B7       JSR  $B7F7
        401B A5 15          LDA  $15
        401D D0 2D          BNE  $404C
        401F A5 14          LDA  $14
```

109

```
4021 8D DB 40        STA $40DB
4024 20 FD AE        JSR $AEFD
4027 20 8A AD        JSR $AD8A
402A 20 F7 B7        JSR $B7F7
402D A5 14           LDA $14
402F 8D DD 40        STA $40DD
4032 A5 15           LDA $15
4034 8D DE 40        STA $40DE
4037 20 FD AE        JSR $AEFD
403A 20 8A AD        JSR $AD8A
403D 20 F7 B7        JSR $B7F7
4040 A5 15           LDA $15
4042 D0 08           BNE $404C
4044 A5 14           LDA $14
4046 8D DC 40        STA $40DC
4049 4C 4F 40        JMP $404F
404C 4C 48 B2        JMP $B248
404F A2 00           LDX #$00
4051 AD DC 40        LDA $40DC
4054 DD DF 40        CMP $40DF,X
4057 F0 08           BEQ $4061
4059 E8              INX
405A E0 04           CPX #$04
405C D0 F6           BNE $4054
405E 4C 4C 40        JMP $404C
4061 AD DA 40        LDA $40DA
4064 F0 E6           BEQ $404C
4066 C9 04           CMP #$04
4068 B0 E2           BCS $404C
406A AD DB 40        LDA $40DB
406D C9 10           CMP #$10
406F B0 DB           BCS $404C
4071 AD DB 40        LDA $40DB
4074 8D 18 D4        STA $D418
4077 AD DA 40        LDA $40DA
407A C9 01           CMP #$01
407C F0 07           BEQ $4085
407E C9 02           CMP #$02
4080 F0 20           BEQ $40A2
4082 4C BF 40        JMP $40BF
4085 AD DC 40        LDA $40DC
```

```
4088 8D 04 D4      STA $D404
408B A9 80         LDA #$80
408D 8D 05 D4      STA $D405
4090 8D 06 D4      STA $D406
4093 AD DD 40      LDA $40DD
4096 8D 00 D4      STA $D400
4099 AD DE 40      LDA $40DE
409C 8D 01 D4      STA $D401
409F 4C D9 40      JMP $40D9
40A2 AD DC 40      LDA $40DC
40A5 8D 0B D4      STA $D40B
40A8 A9 80         LDA #$80
40AA 8D 0C D4      STA $D40C
40AD 8D 0D D4      STA $D40D
40B0 AD DD 40      LDA $40DD
40B3 8D 07 D4      STA $D407
40B6 AD DE 40      LDA $40DE
40B9 8D 08 D4      STA $D408
40BC 4C D9 40      JMP $40D9
40BF AD DC 40      LDA $40DC
40C2 8D 12 D4      STA $D412
40C5 A9 80         LDA #$80
40C7 8D 13 D4      STA $D413
40CA 8D 14 D4      STA $D414
40CD AD DD 40      LDA $40DD
40D0 8D 0E D4      STA $D40E
40D3 AD DE 40      LDA $40DE
40D6 8D 0F D4      STA $D40F
40D9 60            RTS
.
.
.
.
.:40DA 00 00 00 00 00 11 21 41
.:40E2 81 00 BE 00 00 00 F8 00
.
```

28. Envelope

This routine is similair to Sound (above) but it allows you to set the attack, decay, sustain and release as well.

Attack, decay, sustain and release are all betwen 0 and 15.

The syntax is SYS 16384, voice, volume, waveform, frequency, attack, decay, sustain, release.

```
PAL (C)1979 BRAD TEMPLETON
2
20:    4000                            .OPT P,OO
30:    4000                            *=   $4000
                                  ;
                                  ;
                                  ;ENVELOPE FUNCTION
                                  ;
                                  ;SYNTAX
                                  ;
                                  ;SYS16384,VOICE,VOLUME,
                                  ;WAVE,FREQ,A,D,S,R
120:   4000 20 24 41              JSR   GETPARAM
130:   4003 A5 15                 LDA   $15
140:   4005 D0 6D                 BNE   IQERR
150:   4007 A5 14                 LDA   $14
160:   4009 8D 2E 41              STA   VOICE
170:   400C 20 24 41              JSR   GETPARAM
180:   400F A5 15                 LDA   $15
190:   4011 D0 61                 BNE   IQERR
200:   4013 A5 14                 LDA   $14
210:   4015 8D 2F 41              STA   VOLUME
220:   4018 20 24 41              JSR   GETPARAM
230:   401B A5 15                 LDA   $15
240:   401D D0 55                 BNE   IQERR
```

```
250:    401F A5 14              LDA    #14
260:    4021 8D 30 41           STA    WAVE
270:    4024 20 24 41           JSR    GETPARAM
280:    4027 A5 14              LDA    #14
290:    4029 8D 31 41           STA    FREQ
300:    402C A5 15              LDA    #15
310:    402E 8D 32 41           STA    FREQ+1
320:    4031 20 24 41           JSR    GETPARAM
330:    4034 A5 15              LDA    #15
340:    4036 D0 3C              BNE    IQERR
350:    4038 A5 14              LDA    #14
360:    403A C9 10              CMP    #16
370:    403C B0 36              BCS    IQERR
380:    403E 8D 33 41           STA    ATTACK
390:    4041 20 24 41           JSR    GETPARAM
400:    4044 A5 15              LDA    #15
410:    4046 D0 2C              BNE    IQERR
420:    4048 A5 14              LDA    #14
430:    404A C9 10              CMP    #16
440:    404C B0 26              BCS    IQERR
450:    404E 8D 34 41           STA    DECAY
                             ;
470:    4051 20 24 41           JSR    GETPARAM
480:    4054 A5 15              LDA    #15
490:    4056 D0 1C              BNE    IQERR
500:    4058 A5 14              LDA    #14
510:    405A C9 10              CMP    #16
520:    405C B0 16              BCS    IQERR
530:    405E 8D 35 41           STA    SUSTAIN
                             ;
550:    4061 20 24 41           JSR    GETPARAM
560:    4064 A5 15              LDA    #15
570:    4066 D0 0C              BNE    IQERR
580:    4068 A5 14              LDA    #14
590:    406A C9 10              CMP    #16
600:    406C B0 06              BCS    IQERR
610:    406E 8D 36 41           STA    RELEASE
                             ;
630:    4071 4C 77 40           JMP    DO
                             ;
650:    4074 4C 48 B2  IQERR    JMP    #B248
```

113

```
670:    4077 AD 2F 41 DO        LDA   VOLUME
680:    407A C9 10              CMP   #16
690:    407C B0 F6              BCS   IQERR
700:    407E 8D 18 D4           STA   54296
                                ;
                                ;CALCULATE ADSR
                                ;
740:    4081 AD 34 41           LDA   DECAY
750:    4084 4A                 LSR   A
760:    4085 4A                 LSR   A
770:    4086 4A                 LSR   A
780:    4087 4A                 LSR   A
790:    4088 18                 CLC
800:    4089 6D 33 41           ADC   ATTACK
810:    408C 8D 37 41           STA   AD
                                ;
830:    408F AD 36 41           LDA   RELEASE
840:    4092 4A                 LSR   A
850:    4093 4A                 LSR   A
860:    4094 4A                 LSR   A
870:    4095 4A                 LSR   A
880:    4096 18                 CLC
890:    4097 6D 35 41           ADC   SUSTAIN
900:    409A 8D 38 41           STA   SR
                                ;
920:    409D A2 00              LDX   #0
930:    409F AD 30 41           LDA   WAVE
940:    40A2 DD 39 41 LOOP      CMP   WAVETABLE,X
950:    40A5 F0 08              BEQ   MORE
960:    40A7 E8                 INX
960:    40A8 E0 04              CPX   #4
970:    40AA D0 F6              BNE   LOOP
980:    40AC 4C 48 B2 IQERR1    JMP   $B248 ;IQERR
                                ;
1000:   40AF AD 2E 41 MORE      LDA   VOICE
1010:   40B2 F0 F8              BEQ   IQERR1
1020:   40B4 C9 04              CMP   #4
1030:   40B6 B0 F4              BCS   IQERR1
                                ;
1050:   40B8 C9 01              CMP   #1
```

114

```
1060:    40BA F0 07           BEQ    VOICE1
1070:    40BC C9 02           CMP    #2
1080:    40BE F0 24           BEQ    VOICE2
1090:    40C0 4C 05 41        JMP    VOICE3
                          ;
                          ;
1120:    40C3 AD 30 41 VOICE1 LDA    WAVE
1130:    40C6 8D 04 D4        STA    54276
1140:    40C9 AD 37 41        LDA    AD
1150:    40CC 8D 05 D4        STA    54277
1160:    40CF AD 38 41        LDA    SR
1170:    40D2 8D 06 D4        STA    54278
1180:    40D5 AD 31 41        LDA    FREQ
1190:    40D8 8D 00 D4        STA    54272
1200:    40DB AD 32 41        LDA    FREQ+1
1210:    40DE 8D 01 D4        STA    54273
1220:    40E1 4C 23 41        JMP    FINISH
                          ;
1240:    40E4 AD 30 41 VOICE2 LDA    WAVE
1250:    40E7 8D 0B D4        STA    54283
1260:    40EA AD 37 41        LDA    AD
1270:    40ED 8D 0C D4        STA    54284
1280:    40F0 AD 38 41        LDA    SR
1290:    40F3 8D 0D D4        STA    54285
1300:    40F6 AD 31 41        LDA    FREQ
1310:    40F9 8D 07 D4        STA    54279
1320:    40FC AD 32 41        LDA    FREQ+1
1330:    40FF 8D 08 D4        STA    54280
1340:    4102 4C 23 41        JMP    FINISH
                          ;
1360:    4105 AD 30 41 VOICE3 LDA    WAVE
1370:    4108 8D 12 D4        STA    54290
1380:    410B AD 37 41        LDA    AD
1390:    410E 8D 13 D4        STA    54291
1400:    4111 AD 38 41        LDA    SR
1410:    4114 8D 14 D4        STA    54292
1420:    4117 AD 31 41        LDA    FREQ
1430:    411A 8D 0E D4        STA    54286
1440:    411D AD 32 41        LDA    FREQ+1
1450:    4120 8D 0F D4        STA    54287
                          ;
```

```
1480:    4123 60          FINISH    RTS
1490:    4124 20 FD AE    GETPARAM  JSR    #AEFD
1500:    4127 20 8A AD              JSR    #AD8A
1510:    412A 20 F7 B7              JSR    #B7F7
1520:    412D 60                    RTS
1530:    412E 00          VOICE     .BYT 0
1540:    412F 00          VOLUME    .BYT 0
1550:    4130 00          WAVE      .BYT 0
1560:    4131 00 00       FREQ      .WORD0
1570:    4133 00          ATTACK    .BYT 0
1580:    4134 00          DECAY     .BYT 0
1590:    4135 00          SUSTAIN   .BYT 0
1600:    4136 00          RELEASE   .BYT 0
1610:    4137 00          AD        .BYT 0
1620:    4138 00          SR        .BYT 0
1630:    4139 11 21 41    WAVETABLE.BYT 17,33,65,129
]4000-413D

READY.
```

```
B*
      PC   SR AC XR YR SP
.]97FE 72 00 00 01 F6
.
4000 20 24 41        JSR  #4124
4003 A5 15           LDA  #15
4005 D0 6D           BNE  #4074
4007 A5 14           LDA  #14
4009 8D 2E 41        STA  #412E
400C 20 24 41        JSR  #4124
400F A5 15           LDA  #15
4011 D0 61           BNE  #4074
4013 A5 14           LDA  #14
4015 8D 2F 41        STA  #412F
4018 20 24 41        JSR  #4124
```

```
401B  A5 15        LDA #15
401D  D0 55        BNE #4074
401F  A5 14        LDA #14
4021  8D 30 41     STA #4130
4024  20 24 41     JSR #4124
4027  A5 14        LDA #14
4029  8D 31 41     STA #4131
402C  A5 15        LDA #15
402E  8D 32 41     STA #4132
4031  20 24 41     JSR #4124
4034  A5 15        LDA #15
4036  D0 3C        BNE #4074
4038  A5 14        LDA #14
403A  C9 10        CMP ##10
403C  B0 36        BCS #4074
403E  8D 33 41     STA #4133
4041  20 24 41     JSR #4124
4044  A5 15        LDA #15
4046  D0 2C        BNE #4074
4048  A5 14        LDA #14
404A  C9 10        CMP ##10
404C  B0 26        BCS #4074
404E  8D 34 41     STA #4134
4051  20 24 41     JSR #4124
4054  A5 15        LDA #15
4056  D0 1C        BNE #4074
4058  A5 14        LDA #14
405A  C9 10        CMP ##10
405C  B0 16        BCS #4074
405E  8D 35 41     STA #4135
4061  20 24 41     JSR #4124
4064  A5 15        LDA #15
4066  D0 0C        BNE #4074
4068  A5 14        LDA #14
406A  C9 10        CMP ##10
406C  B0 06        BCS #4074
406E  8D 36 41     STA #4136
4071  4C 77 40     JMP #4077
4074  4C 48 B2     JMP #B248
4077  AD 2F 41     LDA #412F
407A  C9 10        CMP ##10
```

```
407C  B0 F6          BCS  $4074
407E  8D 18 D4        STA  $D418
4081  AD 34 41        LDA  $4134
4084  4A              LSR
4085  4A              LSR
4086  4A              LSR
4087  4A              LSR
4088  18              CLC
4089  6D 33 41        ADC  $4133
408C  8D 37 41        STA  $4137
408F  AD 36 41        LDA  $4136
4092  4A              LSR
4093  4A              LSR
4094  4A              LSR
4095  4A              LSR
4096  18              CLC
4097  6D 35 41        ADC  $4135
409A  8D 38 41        STA  $4138
409D  A2 00           LDX  #$00
409F  AD 30 41        LDA  $4130
40A2  DD 39 41        CMP  $4139,X
40A5  F0 08           BEQ  $40AF
40A7  E8              INX
40A8  E0 04           CPX  #$04
40AA  D0 F6           BNE  $40A2
40AC  4C 48 B2        JMP  $B248
40AF  AD 2E 41        LDA  $412E
40B2  F0 F8           BEQ  $40AC
40B4  C9 04           CMP  #$04
40B6  B0 F4           BCS  $40AC
40B8  C9 01           CMP  #$01
40BA  F0 07           BEQ  $40C3
40BC  C9 02           CMP  #$02
40BE  F0 24           BEQ  $40E4
40C0  4C 05 41        JMP  $4105
40C3  AD 30 41        LDA  $4130
40C6  8D 04 D4        STA  $D404
40C9  AD 37 41        LDA  $4137
40CC  8D 05 D4        STA  $D405
40CF  AD 38 41        LDA  $4138
40D2  8D 06 D4        STA  $D406
```

```
40D5 AD 31 41      LDA #4131
40D8 8D 00 D4      STA $D400
40DB AD 32 41      LDA #4132
40DE 8D 01 D4      STA $D401
40E1 4C 23 41      JMP #4123
40E4 AD 30 41      LDA #4130
40E7 8D 0B D4      STA $D40B
40EA AD 37 41      LDA #4137
40ED 8D 0C D4      STA $D40C
40F0 AD 38 41      LDA #4138
40F3 8D 0D D4      STA $D40D
40F6 AD 31 41      LDA #4131
40F9 8D 07 D4      STA $D407
40FC AD 32 41      LDA #4132
40FF 8D 08 D4      STA $D408
4102 4C 23 41      JMP #4123
4105 AD 30 41      LDA #4130
4108 8D 12 D4      STA $D412
410B AD 37 41      LDA #4137
410E 8D 13 D4      STA $D413
4111 AD 38 41      LDA #4138
4114 8D 14 D4      STA $D414
4117 AD 31 41      LDA #4131
411A 8D 0E D4      STA $D40E
411D AD 32 41      LDA #4132
4120 8D 0F D4      STA $D40F
4123 60            RTS
4124 20 FD AE      JSR $AEFD
4127 20 8A AD      JSR $AD8A
412A 20 F7 B7      JSR $B7F7
412D 60            RTS
   .
   .
.:412E 00 00 00 00 00 00 00 00
.:4136 00 00 00 11 21 41 81 04
   .
```

29. DIR

This routine allows you to read the disk directory (of either or both drives on a dual drive (not two 1541s)). It does not disturb the program in memory.

The syntax is SYS 16384,drive

where drive is 0 or 1, or 2 if both drives are to be read.

```
PAL (C)1979 BRAD TEMPLETON
2
20:     3FFD                              .OPT  P,00
30:     3FFD                              *=    16381
40:     3FFD            FNLENGTH  =        $B7
50:     3FFD            SECADR    =        $B9
60:     3FFD            DEVNUM    =        $BA
70:     3FFD            FNADD     =        $BB
80:     3FFD            FNLEN     =        $FD
90:     3FFD            TEMP      =        $FB
100:    3FFD            ST        =        $90
110:    3FFD            SENDFNAM  =        $F3D5
120:    3FFD            CLOSEFIL  =        $F642
130:    3FFD            SENDSEC   =        $FF96
140:    3FFD            IECTALK   =        $FFB4
150:    3FFD            IECINP    =        $FFA5
160:    3FFD            LINENO    =        $BDCD
170:    3FFD            PRINT     =        $FFD2
180:    3FFD            CR        =        13
                        ;
200:    3FFD 4C 48 B2   IQERR     JMP      $B248
                        ;DIR  SYNTAX  SYS 16384
220:    4000 20 FD AE             JSR      $AEFD
230:    4003 20 9E B7             JSR      $B79E
240:    4006 8A                   TXA
```

```
250:    4007 C9 03                    CMP  #3
260:    4009 B0 F2                    BCS  IQERR
270:    400B C9 00                    CMP  #0
270:    400D F0 0F                    BEQ  ZERO
280:    400F C9 01                    CMP  #1
290:    4011 D0 16                    BNE  BOTH
300:    4013 A9 31                    LDA  #"1"
310:    4015 85 FC                    STA  $FC
320:    4017 A9 02                    LDA  #2
330:    4019 85 FD                    STA  FNLEN
340:    401B 4C 2D 40                 JMP  DIR
                              ;
360:    401E            ZERO    =    *
370:    401E A9 30                    LDA  #"0"
380:    4020 85 FC                    STA  $FC
390:    4022 A9 02                    LDA  #2
400:    4024 85 FD                    STA  FNLEN
410:    4026 4C 2D 40                 JMP  DIR
420:    4029 A9 01      BOTH    LDA  #1
430:    402B 85 FD                    STA  FNLEN
                              ;
450:    402D A9 00      DIR     LDA  #0
460:    402F 85 90                    STA  ST
470:    4031 A9 24                    LDA  #"$
480:    4033 85 FB                    STA  TEMP
490:    4035 A9 FB                    LDA  #<TEMP
500:    4037 85 BB                    STA  FNADD
510:    4039 A9 00                    LDA  #>TEMP
520:    403B 85 BC                    STA  FNADD+1
530:    403D A5 FD                    LDA  FNLEN
540:    403F 85 B7                    STA  FNLENGTH
550:    4041 A9 08                    LDA  #8
560:    4043 85 BA                    STA  DEVNUM
570:    4045 A9 60                    LDA  #$60
580:    4047 85 B9                    STA  SECADR
590:    4049 20 D5 F3                 JSR  SENDFNAM
600:    404C A5 BA                    LDA  DEVNUM
610:    404E 20 B4 FF                 JSR  IECTALK
620:    4051 A5 B9                    LDA  SECADR
630:    4053 20 96 FF                 JSR  SENDSEC
640:    4056 A4 90                    LDY  ST
```

```
650:   4058 DØ 3D              BNE   DLIST4
660:   405A AØ 06              LDY   #6
670:   405C 84 FB     DLIST1   STY   TEMP
680:   405E 20 A5 FF           JSR   IECINP
690:   4061 A6 FC              LDX   TEMP+1
700:   4063 85 FC              STA   TEMP+1
710:   4065 A4 90              LDY   ST
720:   4067 DØ 2E              BNE   DLIST4
730:   4069 A4 FB              LDY   TEMP
740:   406B 88                 DEY
750:   406C DØ EE              BNE   DLIST1
760:   406E A4 FC              LDY   TEMP+1
770:   4070 20 CD BD           JSR   LINENO
780:   4073 A9 20              LDA   #$20
790:   4075 20 D2 FF           JSR   PRINT
800:   4078 20 A5 FF DLIST3    JSR   IECINP
810:   407B A6 90              LDX   ST
820:   407D DØ 18              BNE   DLIST4
830:   407F AA                 TAX
840:   4080 FØ 06              BEQ   DLIST2
850:   4082 20 D2 FF           JSR   PRINT
860:   4085 4C 78 40           JMP   DLIST3
870:   4088 A9 ØD     DLIST2   LDA   #CR
880:   408A 20 D2 FF           JSR   PRINT
890:   408D A5 C5              LDA   $C5
900:   408F C9 3F              CMP   #63
900:   4091 FØ 04              BEQ   DLIST4
910:   4093 AØ 04              LDY   #4
920:   4095 DØ C5              BNE   DLIST1
930:   4097 20 42 F6 DLIST4    JSR   CLOSEFIL
940:   409A 60                 RTS
]3FFD-409B

READY.
```

```
B*
    PC   SR AC XR YR SP
.I97FE 72 ØØ ØØ Øl F6
.
4ØØØ 2Ø FD AE        JSR *AEFD
4ØØ3 2Ø 9E B7        JSR *B79E
4ØØ6 8A              TXA
4ØØ7 C9 Ø3           CMP #*Ø3
4ØØ9 BØ F2           BCS *3FFD
4ØØB C9 ØØ           CMP #*ØØ
4ØØD FØ ØF           BEQ *4Ø1E
4ØØF C9 Ø1           CMP #*Ø1
4Ø11 DØ 16           BNE *4Ø29
4Ø13 A9 31           LDA #*31
4Ø15 85 FC           STA *FC
4Ø17 A9 Ø2           LDA #*Ø2
4Ø19 85 FD           STA *FD
4Ø1B 4C 2D 4Ø        JMP *4Ø2D
4Ø1E A9 3Ø           LDA #*3Ø
4Ø2Ø 85 FC           STA *FC
4Ø22 A9 Ø2           LDA #*Ø2
4Ø24 85 FD           STA *FD
4Ø26 4C 2D 4Ø        JMP *4Ø2D
4Ø29 A9 Ø1           LDA #*Ø1
4Ø2B 85 FD           STA *FD
4Ø2D A9 ØØ           LDA #*ØØ
4Ø2F 85 9Ø           STA *9Ø
4Ø31 A9 24           LDA #*24
4Ø33 85 FB           STA *FB
4Ø35 A9 FB           LDA #*FB
4Ø37 85 BB           STA *BB
4Ø39 A9 ØØ           LDA #*ØØ
4Ø3B 85 BC           STA *BC
4Ø3D A5 FD           LDA *FD
4Ø3F 85 B7           STA *B7
4Ø41 A9 Ø8           LDA #*Ø8
4Ø43 85 BA           STA *BA
4Ø45 A9 6Ø           LDA #*6Ø
4Ø47 85 B9           STA *B9
4Ø49 2Ø D5 F3        JSR *F3D5
4Ø4C A5 BA           LDA *BA
```

```
404E 20 B4 FF      JSR $FFB4
4051 A5 B9         LDA $B9
4053 20 96 FF      JSR $FF96
4056 A4 90         LDY $90
4058 D0 3D         BNE $4097
405A A0 06         LDY #$06
405C 84 FB         STY $FB
405E 20 A5 FF      JSR $FFA5
4061 A6 FC         LDX $FC
4063 85 FC         STA $FC
4065 A4 90         LDY $90
4067 D0 2E         BNE $4097
4069 A4 FB         LDY $FB
406B 88            DEY
406C D0 EE         BNE $405C
406E A4 FC         LDY $FC
4070 20 CD BD      JSR $BDCD
4073 A9 20         LDA #$20
4075 20 D2 FF      JSR $FFD2
4078 20 A5 FF      JSR $FFA5
407B A6 90         LDX $90
407D D0 18         BNE $4097
407F AA            TAX
4080 F0 06         BEQ $4088
4082 20 D2 FF      JSR $FFD2
4085 4C 78 40      JMP $4078
4088 A9 0D         LDA #$0D
408A 20 D2 FF      JSR $FFD2
408D A5 C5         LDA $C5
408F C9 3F         CMP #$3F
4091 F0 04         BEQ $4097
4093 A0 04         LDY #$04
4095 D0 C5         BNE $405C
4097 20 42 F6      JSR $F642
409A 60            RTS
```

30. MSAVE

The following routine allows you save any specified area of
memory. You specify the filename, the device, the secondary
address, the start address and the finishing address + 1.

The syntax is as follows:

SYS 16384,"name",device,1,start,finish + 1

```
PAL  (C)1979 BRAD TEMPLETON
2
20:      4000                           .OPT P,OO
30:      4000                           *=    $4000
                               I
50:      4000 20 FD AE           JSR   $AEFD
60:      4003 20 D4 E1           JSR   $E1D4
70:      4006 20 FD AE           JSR   $AEFD
80:      4009 20 8A AD           JSR   $AD8A
90:      400C 20 F7 B7           JSR   $B7F7
100:     400F A5 14              LDA   $14
110:     4011 48                 PHA
120:     4012 A5 15              LDA   $15
130:     4014 48                 PHA
140:     4015 20 FD AE           JSR   $AEFD
150:     4018 20 8A AD           JSR   $AD8A
160:     401B 20 F7 B7           JSR   $B7F7
170:     401E A6 14              LDX   $14
180:     4020 A4 15              LDY   $15
190:     4022 68                 PLA
200:     4023 85 FC              STA   $FC
210:     4025 68                 PLA
220:     4026 85 FB              STA   $FB
```

```
230:    4028 A9 FB              LDA  #$FB
240:    402A 4C 5F E1           JMP  $E15F
]4000-402D

READY.
```

```
B*
    PC  SR AC XR YR SP
.197FE 72 00 00 01 F6
.
.
4000 20 FD AE      JSR $AEFD
4003 20 D4 E1      JSR $E1D4
4006 20 FD AE      JSR $AEFD
4009 20 8A AD      JSR $AD8A
400C 20 F7 B7      JSR $B7F7
400F A5 14         LDA $14
4011 48            PHA
4012 A5 15         LDA $15
4014 48            PHA
4015 20 FD AE      JSR $AEFD
4018 20 8A AD      JSR $AD8A
401B 20 F7 B7      JSR $B7F7
401E A6 14         LDX $14
4020 A4 15         LDY $15
4022 68            PLA
4023 85 FC         STA $FC
4025 68            PLA
4026 85 FB         STA $FB
4028 A9 FB         LDA #$FB
402A 4C 5F E1      JMP $E15F
.
```

31. MLOAD/MVERIFY

The following routine allows you to load or verify to or from a specified area of memory. The load enables you to load into any area of memory, whether it was saved from that area or not. The verify allows you to verify a specific area of memory.

The syntax for MLOAD is as follows:

SYS 16394,"name",device,1,start address

The syntax for MVERIFY is as follows:

SYS 16384,"name",device,1,start

```
PAL  (C)1979 BRAD TEMPLETON
2
20:      4000                        .OPT P,00
30:      4000                        *=    $4000
40:      4000 20 FD AE MVERIFY  JSR   $AEFD
50:      4003 A9 01              LDA   #1
60:      4005 85 0A              STA   $A
70:      4007 4C 11 40           JMP   LO
80:      400A 20 FD AE MLOAD    JSR   $AEFD
90:      400D A9 00              LDA   #0
100:     400F 85 0A              STA   $A
110:     4011 20 D4 E1 LO       JSR   $E1D4
120:     4014 20 FD AE           JSR   $AEFD
130:     4017 20 8A AD           JSR   $AD8A
140:     401A 20 F7 B7           JSR   $B7F7
150:     401D A5 0A              LDA   $A
160:     401F A6 14              LDX   $14
170:     4021 A4 15              LDY   $15
180:     4023 4C 75 E1           JMP   $E175
]4000-4026

READY.
```

127

```
B*
    PC   SR AC XR YR SP
.197FE 72 00 00 01 F6
.
4000 20 FD AE       JSR $AEFD
4003 A9 01          LDA #$01
4005 85 0A          STA $0A
4007 4C 11 40       JMP $4011
400A 20 FD AE       JSR $AEFD
400D A9 00          LDA #$00
400F 85 0A          STA $0A
4011 20 D4 E1       JSR $E1D4
4014 20 FD AE       JSR $AEFD
4017 20 8A AD       JSR $AD8A
401A 20 F7 B7       JSR $B7F7
401D A5 0A          LDA $0A
401F A6 14          LDX $14
4021 A4 15          LDY $15
4023 4C 75 E1       JMP $E175
```

32. Disk

This routine allows you to send a command to the command channel of the disk drive, e.g. initialise or format.

It replaces the following in Basic:

OPEN15,8,15,"COMMAND"

The syntax is as follows:

SYS 16384,"command"

```
PAL (C)1979 BRAD TEMPLETON
2
 20:    4000                        .OPT P,00
 30:    4000                        *=    $4000
                            ; SYNTAX SYS16384,
                            ; "COMMAND"
 60:    4000         CLOSE    =    $FFC3
 70:    4000         OPEN     =    $FFC0
 80:    4000         GETNAME  =    $E257
 90:    4000         NEXTQ    =    $E206
100:    4000         SETFNA   =    $FFBD
110:    4000         SETFPA   =    $FFBA
120:    4000         GIVERR   =    $E0F9
                            ;
140:    4000 20 FD AE        JSR    $AEFD
150:    4003 A9 0F           LDA    #15
160:    4005 20 C3 FF        JSR    CLOSE
170:    4008 20 16 40        JSR    GETFPAR
180:    400B 20 C0 FF        JSR    OPEN
190:    400E B0 1A           BCS    ERROR
200:    4010 A9 0F           LDA    #15
210:    4012 20 C3 FF        JSR    CLOSE
```

```
220:      4015 60                          RTS
                             I
240:      4016 A9 00         GETFPAR  LDA  #0
250:      4018 20 BD FF               JSR  SETFNA
260:      401B A9 0F                  LDA  #15
270:      401D A8                     TAY
280:      401E A2 08                  LDX  #8
290:      4020 20 BA FF               JSR  SETFPA
300:      4023 20 06 E2               JSR  NEXTQ
310:      4026 20 57 E2               JSR  GETNAME
320:      4029 60                     RTS
330:      402A 4C F9 E0 ERROR         JMP  GIVERR
14000-402D
```

READY.


```
    B*
         PC   SR AC XR YR SP
    .|97FE 72 00 00 01 F6
    .
    4000 20 FD AE      JSR $AEFD
    4003 A9 0F         LDA #$0F
    4005 20 C3 FF      JSR $FFC3
    4008 20 16 40      JSR $4016
    400B 20 C0 FF      JSR $FFC0
    400E B0 1A         BCS $402A
    4010 A9 0F         LDA #$0F
    4012 20 C3 FF      JSR $FFC3
    4015 60            RTS
    4016 A9 00         LDA #$00
    4018 20 BD FF      JSR $FFBD
    401B A9 0F         LDA #$0F
    401D A8            TAY
    401E A2 08         LDX #$08
    4020 20 BA FF      JSR $FFBA
    4023 20 06 E2      JSR $E206
    4026 20 57 E2      JSR $E257
    4029 60            RTS
    402A 4C F9 E0      JMP $E0F9
    .
```

33. DERROR

This routine allows you to read the disk error channel in direct mode or during a program.

It replaces the following BASIC program:

```
10 OPEN15,8,15
20 INPUT # 15,A$,B$,C$,D$,E$
30 PRINT A$;B$;C$;D$;E$
40 CLOSE15
```

The syntax is SYS 16384

```
PAL (C)1979 BRAD TEMPLETON
2
20:    4000                        .OPT P,00
30:    4000                        *=    $4000
40:    4000          ST      =     $90
50:    4000          DEVNUM  =     $BA
60:    4000          SECADR  =     $B9
70:    4000          IECTALK =     $FFB4
80:    4000          SENDSEC =     $FF96
90:    4000          IECINP  =     $FFA5
100:   4000          PRINT   =     $FFD2
110:   4000          UNTALK  =     $FFAB
                     ;
                     ;DERROR COMMAND
                     ;
150:   4000 A9 00    LDA   #0
160:   4002 85 90    STA   ST
170:   4004 A9 08    LDA   #8
180:   4006 85 BA    STA   DEVNUM
190:   4008 20 B4 FF JSR   IECTALK
200:   400B A9 6F    LDA   #$6F
```

```
210:     400D 85 B9                STA    SECADR
220:     400F 20 96 FF             JSR    SENDSEC
230:     4012 A4 90      LOOP      LDY    ST
240:     4014 D0 0A                BNE    DERR4
250:     4016 20 A5 FF             JSR    IECINP
260:     4019 20 D2 FF             JSR    PRINT
270:     401C C9 0D                CMP    #13
280:     401E D0 F2                BNE    LOOP
290:     4020 20 AB FF DERR4       JSR    UNTALK
300:     4023 60                   RTS
]4000-4024

READY.
```

```
B*
      PC   SR AC XR YR SP
.;97FE 72 00 00 01 F6
.
4000 A9 00              LDA  #$00
4002 85 90              STA  $90
4004 A9 08              LDA  #$08
4006 85 BA              STA  $BA
4008 20 B4 FF           JSR  $FFB4
400B A9 6F              LDA  #$6F
400D 85 B9              STA  $B9
400F 20 96 FF           JSR  $FF96
4012 A4 90              LDY  $90
4014 D0 0A              BNE  $4020
4016 20 A5 FF           JSR  $FFA5
4019 20 D2 FF           JSR  $FFD2
401C C9 0D              CMP  #$0D
401E D0 F2              BNE  $4012
4020 20 AB FF           JSR  $FFAB
4023 60                 RTS
.
```

34. Scroll message

This routine allows a message to be scrolled across the screen independently of anything else. This could be useful during the introduction to a game, for example.

The text to be scrolled across can be any length from 1 character onwards. The text must end with a $FF (255) byte to tell the routine to start from the beginning again.

Three parameters are required by the routine: the start location of the text in memory, the rate of scrolling and the colour of the text. If for example you wanted one new letter to appear on the screen once every sixth of a second then the rate would be 10 (as 10/60 is one sixth).

The syntax is as follows:

    SYS 16384,start of text,rate,colour

```
PAL  (C)1979  BRAD TEMPLETON
2
20:    4000                          .OPT  P,00
30:    4000                          *=    $4000

                            ;
50:    4000 20 FD AE                  JSR   $AEFD

60:    4003 20 8A AD                  JSR   $AD8A

70:    4006 20 F7 B7                  JSR   $B7F7

                            ;
90:    4009 A5 14                     LDA   $14
100:   400B 85 FB                     STA   $FB
```

```
100:    400D 8D 96 40              STA    TEMPF
B
110:    4010 A5 15                 LDA    $15
120:    4012 85 FC                 STA    $FC
120:    4014 8D 97 40              STA    TEMPF
C
                             ;
140:    4017 20 FD AE              JSR    $AEFD

150:    401A 20 9E B7              JSR    $B79E

160:    401D 8A                    TXA
170:    401E 8D 95 40              STA    TEMP
180:    4021 8D 94 40              STA    COUNT
ER
190:    4024 20 FD AE              JSR    $AEFD

200:    4027 20 9E B7              JSR    $B79E

210:    402A 8E 98 40              STX    COLOU
R
                             ;
230:    402D 78                    SEI
240:    402E A9 3A                 LDA    #<MAI
N
250:    4030 8D 14 03              STA    788
260:    4033 A9 40                 LDA    #>MAI
N
270:    4035 8D 15 03              STA    789
280:    4038 58                    CLI
290:    4039 60                    RTS
                             ;
                             ;
320:    403A CE 94 40 MAIN         DEC    COUNT
ER
330:    403D D0 38                 BNE    FINIS
H
                             ;
350:    403F AD 95 40              LDA    TEMP
360:    4042 8D 94 40              STA    COUNT
ER
```

```
370:     4045 A2 00              LDX    #0
380:     4047 BD 99 07 LOOP      LDA    1945,
X
390:     404A 9D 98 07           STA    1944,
X
400:     404D BD 99 DB           LDA    1945+
54272,X
410:     4050 9D 98 DB           STA    1944+
54272,X
420:     4053 E8                 INX
430:     4054 E0 27              CPX    #39
440:     4056 D0 EF              BNE    LOOP
                           ;
460:     4058 A0 00              LDY    #0
470:     405A B1 FB              LDA    ($FB)
,Y
480:     405C C9 3F              CMP    #63
481:     405E B0 03              BCS    SUBTR

482:     4060 4C 66 40           JMP    PUTON

483:     4063 38       SUBTR     SEC
484:     4064 E9 40              SBC    #64
500:     4066 8D BF 07 PUTON     STA    1983
510:     4069 20 7A 40           JSR    INCRE
MENT
520:     406C A5 FC              LDA    $FC
530:     406E 18                 CLC
540:     406F 69 D4              ADC    #212
550:     4071 AD 98 40           LDA    COLOU
R
560:     4074 8D BF DB           STA    1983+
54272
                           ;
580:     4077 4C 31 EA FINISH    JMP    $EA31

590:     407A E6 FB    INCREMENTINC    $FB
600:     407C D0 02              BNE    CHECK

610:     407E E6 FC              INC    $FC
                           ;
```

```
630:      4080 A0 00      CHECK     LDY  #0
640:      4082 B1 FB                LDA  ($FB)
,Y
650:      4084 C9 FF                CMP  #$FF
660:      4086 F0 01                BEQ  RESET

670:      4088 60                   RTS
680:      4089 AD 96 40 RESET       LDA  TEMPF
B
690:      408C 85 FB                STA  $FB
700:      408E AD 97 40             LDA  TEMPF
C
710:      4091 85 FC                STA  $FC
720:      4093 60                   RTS
730:      4094 00       COUNTER     .BYT 0
740:      4095 00       TEMP        .BYT 0
750:      4096 00       TEMPFB      .BYT 0
760:      4097 00       TEMPFC      .BYT 0
770:      4098 00       COLOUR      .BYT 0
780:      4099 48 45 4C             .ASC "HELL
O I AM A CBM 64 MICRO-"
790:      40B3 43 4F 4D             .ASC "COMP
UTER AND I AM 64 "
800:      40C8 FF                   .BYT $FF
]4000-40C9
```

```
B*
     PC  SR AC XR YR SP
.;97FE 72 00 00 40 F6

.
4000 20 FD AE       JSR  $AEFD
4003 20 8A AD       JSR  $AD8A
4006 20 F7 B7       JSR  $B7F7
4009 A5 14          LDA  $14
400B 85 FB          STA  $FB
400D 8D 96 40       STA  $4096
4010 A5 15          LDA  $15
4012 85 FC          STA  $FC
```

136

```
4014 8D 97 40      STA $4097
4017 20 FD AE      JSR $AEFD
401A 20 9E B7      JSR $B79E
401D 8A            TXA
401E 8D 95 40      STA $4095
4021 8D 94 40      STA $4094
4024 20 FD AE      JSR $AEFD
4027 20 9E B7      JSR $B79E
402A 8E 98 40      STX $4098
402D 78            SEI
402E A9 3A         LDA #$3A
4030 8D 14 03      STA $0314
4033 A9 40         LDA #$40
4035 8D 15 03      STA $0315
4038 58            CLI
4039 60            RTS
403A CE 94 40      DEC $4094
403D D0 38         BNE $4077
403F AD 95 40      LDA $4095
4042 8D 94 40      STA $4094
4045 A2 00         LDX #$00
4047 BD 99 07      LDA $0799,X
404A 9D 98 07      STA $0798,X
404D BD 99 DB      LDA $DB99,X
4050 9D 98 DB      STA $DB98,X
4053 E8            INX
4054 E0 27         CPX #$27
4056 D0 EF         BNE $4047
4058 A0 00         LDY #$00
405A B1 FB         LDA ($FB),Y
405C C9 3F         CMP #$3F
405E B0 03         BCS $4063
4060 4C 66 40      JMP $4066
4063 38            SEC
4064 E9 40         SBC #$40
4066 8D BF 07      STA $07BF
4069 20 7A 40      JSR $407A
406C A5 FC         LDA $FC
406E 18            CLC
406F 69 D4         ADC #$D4
4071 AD 98 40      LDA $4098
```

137

```
4074 8D BF DB      STA $DBBF
4077 4C 31 EA      JMP $EA31
407A E6 FB         INC $FB
407C DØ Ø2         BNE $4080
407E E6 FC         INC $FC
4080 AØ ØØ         LDY #$00
4082 B1 FB         LDA ($FB),Y
4084 C9 FF         CMP #$FF
4086 FØ Ø1         BEQ $4089
4088 6Ø            RTS
4089 AD 96 4Ø      LDA $4096
408C 85 FB         STA $FB
408E AD 97 4Ø      LDA $4097
4091 85 FC         STA $FC
4093 6Ø            RTS
 .


 .
.:4094 ØØ ØØ ØØ ØØ ØØ 48 45 4C
.:409C 4C 4F 2Ø 49 2Ø 41 4D 2Ø
.:40A4 41 2Ø 43 42 4D 2Ø 36 34
.:40AC 2Ø 4D 49 43 52 4F 2D 43
.:40B4 4F 4D 5Ø 55 54 45 52 2Ø
.:40BC 41 4E 44 2Ø 49 2Ø 41 4D
.:40C4 2Ø 36 34 2Ø FF AD 37 41
 .
```

35. Flash screen

This routine allows you to flash the screen colour from one colour to another at a specified rate.

The syntax is as follows:

SYS 16384,colour1,colour2,rate

where colour1 is the first colour, colour2 is the second and rate is the number of 60ths of a second between flashes, e.g. 10 is 1/6 second. Setting the rate to 0 switches off the flash.

```
PAL (C)1979 BRAD TEMPLETON
2
20:     4000                          .OPT P,00
30:     4000                          *=     $4000
                             ; SYNTAX
                             ; SYSFLASH,COLOUR1,
                             ; COLOUR2,NO OF
                             ; CHANGES A SECOND
50:     4000 20 FD AE            JSR    $AEFD
70:     4003 20 8A AD            JSR    $AD8A
80:     4006 20 F7 B7            JSR    $B7F7
90:     4009 A5 15               LDA    $15
90:     400B F0 03               BEQ    MORE
90:     400D 4C 48 B2            JMP    $B248
100:    4010 A5 14      MORE     LDA    $14
101:    4012 8D 8E 40            STA    TEMP
102:    4015 20 FD AE            JSR    $AEFD
110:    4018 20 8A AD            JSR    $AD8A
120:    401B 20 F7 B7            JSR    $B7F7
130:    401E A5 15               LDA    $15
```

```
140:    4020 FØ Ø3              BEQ  MORE1
150:    4022 4C 48 B2           JMP  $B248
160:    4025 A5 14      MORE1   LDA  $14
170:    4027 8D 8F 40           STA  TEMP+1
180:    402A 20 FD AE           JSR  $AEFD
190:    402D 20 8A AD           JSR  $AD8A
200:    4030 20 F7 B7           JSR  $B7F7
210:    4033 A5 15             LDA  $15
220:    4035 FØ Ø3              BEQ  MORE2
230:    4037 4C 48 B2           JMP  $B248
240:    403A A5 14      MORE2   LDA  $14
240:    403C FØ 43             BEQ  RESET
250:    403E 8D 90 40           STA  TEMP+2
250:    4041 78                 SEI
260:    4042 A9 54             LDA  #<MAIN
270:    4044 8D 14 Ø3           STA  788
280:    4047 A9 40             LDA  #>MAIN
290:    4049 8D 15 Ø3           STA  789
300:    404C 58                 CLI
310:    404D AD 90 40           LDA  TEMP+2
310:    4050 8D 91 40           STA  TEMP+3
320:    4053 60                 RTS
330:    4054           MAIN    =    *
340:    4054 CE 91 40           DEC  TEMP+3
350:    4057 DØ 25              BNE  FINISH
360:    4059 AD 21 DØ           LDA  53281
360:    405C 29 ØF             AND  #15
370:    405E CD 8F 40           CMP  TEMP+1
380:    4061 FØ ØF             BEQ  DOØ
390:    4063 AD 8F 40           LDA  TEMP+1
400:    4066 8D 21 DØ           STA  53281
400:    4069 AD 90 40           LDA  TEMP+2
400:    406C 8D 91 40           STA  TEMP+3
410:    406F 4C 7E 40           JMP  FINISH
420:    4072 AD 8E 40  DOØ     LDA  TEMP
430:    4075 8D 21 DØ           STA  53281
440:    4078 AD 90 40           LDA  TEMP+2
440:    407B 8D 91 40           STA  TEMP+3
450:    407E 4C 31 EA  FINISH  JMP  $EA31
460:    4081 78        RESET   SEI
470:    4082 A9 31             LDA  #49
```

```
480:     4084 8D 14 03           STA    788
490:     4087 A9 EA              LDA    #234
500:     4089 8D 15 03           STA    789
510:     408C 58                 CLI
520:     408D 60                 RTS
530:     408E          TEMP      =      *
]4000-408E

READY.



B*
     PC   SR AC XR YR SP
.}97FE 72 00 00 40 F6

.
4000 20 FD AE         JSR  $AEFD
4003 20 8A AD         JSR  $AD8A
4006 20 F7 B7         JSR  $B7F7
4009 A5 15            LDA  $15
400B F0 03            BEQ  $4010
400D 4C 48 B2         JMP  $B248
4010 A5 14            LDA  $14
4012 8D 8E 40         STA  $408E
4015 20 FD AE         JSR  $AEFD
4018 20 8A AD         JSR  $AD8A
401B 20 F7 B7         JSR  $B7F7
401E A5 15            LDA  $15
4020 F0 03            BEQ  $4025
4022 4C 48 B2         JMP  $B248
4025 A5 14            LDA  $14
4027 8D 8F 40         STA  $408F
402A 20 FD AE         JSR  $AEFD
402D 20 8A AD         JSR  $AD8A
4030 20 F7 B7         JSR  $B7F7
4033 A5 15            LDA  $15
4035 F0 03            BEQ  $403A
4037 4C 48 B2         JMP  $B248
```

141

```
403A  A5 14        LDA $14
403C  F0 43        BEQ $4081
403E  8D 90 40     STA $4090
4041  78           SEI
4042  A9 54        LDA #$54
4044  8D 14 03     STA $0314
4047  A9 40        LDA #$40
4049  8D 15 03     STA $0315
404C  58           CLI
404D  AD 90 40     LDA $4090
4050  8D 91 40     STA $4091
4053  60           RTS
4054  CE 91 40     DEC $4091
4057  D0 25        BNE $407E
4059  AD 21 D0     LDA $D021
405C  29 0F        AND #$0F
405E  CD 8F 40     CMP $408F
4061  F0 0F        BEQ $4072
4063  AD 8F 40     LDA $408F
4066  8D 21 D0     STA $D021
4069  AD 90 40     LDA $4090
406C  8D 91 40     STA $4091
406F  4C 7E 40     JMP $407E
4072  AD 8E 40     LDA $408E
4075  8D 21 D0     STA $D021
4078  AD 90 40     LDA $4090
407B  8D 91 40     STA $4091
407E  4C 31 EA     JMP $EA31
4081  78           SEI
4082  A9 31        LDA #$31
4084  8D 14 03     STA $0314
4087  A9 EA        LDA #$EA
4089  8D 15 03     STA $0315
408C  58           CLI
408D  60           RTS
```
.

36. Flash border

This routine does the same as the flash screen routine except that the border is flashed.

The syntax is as follows:

SYS16384,colour1,colour2,rate

Setting the rate to 0 turns off the flash.

```
PAL (C)1979 BRAD TEMPLETON
2
20:      4000                            .OPT P,OO
30:      4000                            *=    $4000
                              ; SYNTAX
                              ; SYSFLASH,COLOUR1,
                              ; COLOUR2,NO OF
                              ; CHANGES A SECOND
50:      4000 20 FD AE                 JSR   $AEFD
70:      4003 20 8A AD                 JSR   $AD8A
80:      4006 20 F7 B7                 JSR   $B7F7
90:      4009 A5 15                    LDA   $15
90:      400B F0 03                    BEQ   MORE
90:      400D 4C 48 B2                 JMP   $B248
100:     4010 A5 14      MORE          LDA   $14
101:     4012 8D 8E 40                 STA   TEMP
102:     4015 20 FD AE                 JSR   $AEFD
110:     4018 20 8A AD                 JSR   $AD8A
120:     401B 20 F7 B7                 JSR   $B7F7
130:     401E A5 15                    LDA   $15
140:     4020 F0 03                    BEQ   MORE1
150:     4022 4C 48 B2                 JMP   $B248
```

143

```
160:    4025 A5 14       MORE1    LDA    $14
170:    4027 8D 8F 40              STA    TEMP+1
180:    402A 20 FD AE              JSR    $AEFD
190:    402D 20 8A AD              JSR    $AD8A
200:    4030 20 F7 B7              JSR    $B7F7
210:    4033 A5 15                 LDA    $15
220:    4035 F0 03                 BEQ    MORE2
230:    4037 4C 48 B2              JMP    $B248
240:    403A A5 14       MORE2    LDA    $14
240:    403C F0 43                 BEQ    RESET
250:    403E 8D 90 40              STA    TEMP+2
250:    4041 78                    SEI
260:    4042 A9 54                 LDA    #<MAIN
270:    4044 8D 14 03              STA    788
280:    4047 A9 40                 LDA    #>MAIN
290:    4049 8D 15 03              STA    789
300:    404C 58                    CLI
310:    404D AD 90 40              LDA    TEMP+2
310:    4050 8D 91 40              STA    TEMP+3
320:    4053 60                    RTS
330:    4054            MAIN      =      *
340:    4054 CE 91 40              DEC    TEMP+3
350:    4057 D0 25                 BNE    FINISH
360:    4059 AD 20 D0              LDA    53280
360:    405C 29 0F                 AND    #15
370:    405E CD 8F 40              CMP    TEMP+1
380:    4061 F0 0F                 BEQ    DO0
390:    4063 AD 8F 40              LDA    TEMP+1
400:    4066 8D 20 D0              STA    53280
400:    4069 AD 90 40              LDA    TEMP+2
400:    406C 8D 91 40              STA    TEMP+3
410:    406F 4C 7E 40              JMP    FINISH
420:    4072 AD 8E 40   DO0       LDA    TEMP
430:    4075 8D 20 D0              STA    53280
440:    4078 AD 90 40              LDA    TEMP+2
440:    407B 8D 91 40              STA    TEMP+3
450:    407E 4C 31 EA   FINISH    JMP    $EA31
460:    4081 78         RESET     SEI
470:    4082 A9 31                 LDA    #49
480:    4084 8D 14 03              STA    788
490:    4087 A9 EA                 LDA    #234
```

144

```
500:      4089 8D 15 03           STA  789
510:      408C 58                 CLI
520:      408D 60                 RTS
530:      408E           TEMP     =    *
]4000-408E

READY.




          B*
              PC  SR AC XR YR SP
          .}97FE 72 00 00 40 F6
          .
          4000 20 FD AE     JSR $AEFD
          4003 20 8A AD     JSR $AD8A
          4006 20 F7 B7     JSR $B7F7
          4009 A5 15        LDA $15
          400B F0 03        BEQ $4010
          400D 4C 48 B2     JMP $B248
          4010 A5 14        LDA $14
          4012 8D 8E 40     STA $408E
          4015 20 FD AE     JSR $AEFD
          4018 20 8A AD     JSR $AD8A
          401B 20 F7 B7     JSR $B7F7
          401E A5 15        LDA $15
          4020 F0 03        BEQ $4025
          4022 4C 48 B2     JMP $B248
          4025 A5 14        LDA $14
          4027 8D 8F 40     STA $408F
          402A 20 FD AE     JSR $AEFD
          402D 20 8A AD     JSR $AD8A
          4030 20 F7 B7     JSR $B7F7
          4033 A5 15        LDA $15
          4035 F0 03        BEQ $403A
          4037 4C 48 B2     JMP $B248
          403A A5 14        LDA $14
          403C F0 43        BEQ $4081
          403E 8D 90 40     STA $4090
```

```
4041 78              SEI
4042 A9 54           LDA #$54
4044 8D 14 03        STA $0314
4047 A9 40           LDA #$40
4049 8D 15 03        STA $0315
404C 58              CLI
404D AD 90 40        LDA $4090
4050 8D 91 40        STA $4091
4053 60              RTS
4054 CE 91 40        DEC $4091
4057 D0 25           BNE $407E
4059 AD 20 D0        LDA $D020
405C 29 0F           AND #$0F
405E CD 8F 40        CMP $408F
4061 F0 0F           BEQ $4072
4063 AD 8F 40        LDA $408F
4066 8D 20 D0        STA $D020
4069 AD 90 40        LDA $4090
406C 8D 91 40        STA $4091
406F 4C 7E 40        JMP $407E
4072 AD 8E 40        LDA $408E
4075 8D 20 D0        STA $D020
4078 AD 90 40        LDA $4090
407B 8D 91 40        STA $4091
407E 4C 31 EA        JMP $EA31
4081 78              SEI
4082 A9 31           LDA #$31
4084 8D 14 03        STA $0314
4087 A9 EA           LDA #$EA
4089 8D 15 03        STA $0315
408C 58              CLI
408D 60              RTS
.
```

37. Flash characters

This routine flashes (or reverses) all the characters on the screen at a specified rate.

The syntax is as follows:

SYS 16384,rate

Setting the rate to 0 turns off the flash.

```
PAL  (C)1979  BRAD TEMPLETON
2
20:     4000                        .OPT P,00
30:     4000                        *=   $4000

                        ;
                        ;SYNTAX FLASH 1 OR
                        ;0
                        ;
70:     4000 20 FD AE              JSR   $AEFD

80:     4003 20 8A AD              JSR   $AD8A

90:     4006 20 F7 B7              JSR   $B7F7

100:    4009 A5 14                 LDA   $14
110:    400B F0 13                 BEQ   RESET

120:    400D 8D 67 40              STA   TEMP
120:    4010 8D 68 40              STA   TEMP+
1
130:    4013 78                    SEI
140:    4014 A9 2D                 LDA   #<MAI
N
```

```
150:      4016 8D 14 03           STA   788
160:      4019 A9 40              LDA   #>MAI
N
170:      401B 8D 15 03           STA   789
180:      401E 58                 CLI
190:      401F 60                 RTS
200:      4020 78          RESET  SEI
220:      4021 A9 31              LDA   #49
230:      4023 8D 14 03           STA   788
240:      4026 A9 EA              LDA   #234
250:      4028 8D 15 03           STA   789
260:      402B 58                 CLI
270:      402C 60                 RTS
290:      402D CE 68 40 MAIN      DEC   TEMP+
1
300:      4030 F0 03              BEQ   MORE
310:      4032 4C 31 EA           JMP   $EA31

320:      4035 AD 67 40 MORE      LDA   TEMP
330:      4038 8D 68 40           STA   TEMP+
1
                          ;
                          ; INVERT CHARACTERS

                          ;
370:      403B A2 00              LDX   #0
380:      403D BD 00 04 LOOP      LDA   1024,
X
390:      4040 18                 CLC
400:      4041 69 80              ADC   #128
410:      4043 9D 00 04           STA   1024,
X
                          ;
430:      4046 BD FF 04           LDA   1024+
255,X
440:      4049 18                 CLC
450:      404A 69 80              ADC   #128
460:      404C 9D FF 04           STA   1024+
255,X
                          ;
480:      404F BD FE 05           LDA   1024+
```

148

```
255+255,X
490:     4052 18                        CLC
500:     4053 69 80                     ADC   #128
510:     4055 9D FE 05                  STA   1024+
255+255,X
                               ;
530:     4058 BD FD 06                  LDA   1024+
255+255+255,X
540:     405B 18                        CLC
550:     405C 69 80                     ADC   #128
560:     405E 9D FD 06                  STA   1024+
255+255+255,X
570:     4061 E8                        INX
580:     4062 D0 D9                     BNE   LOOP
590:     4064 4C 31 EA                  JMP   $EA31

600:     4067            TEMP      =     *
14000-4067


READY.




        B*
            PC  SR AC XR YR SP
        .197FE 72 00 00 40 F6

        .
        4000 20 FD AE      JSR $AEFD
        4003 20 8A AD      JSR $AD8A
        4006 20 F7 B7      JSR $B7F7
        4009 A5 14         LDA $14
        400B F0 13         BEQ $4020
        400D 8D 67 40      STA $4067
        4010 8D 68 40      STA $4068
        4013 78            SEI
        4014 A9 2D         LDA #$2D
        4016 8D 14 03      STA $0314
        4019 A9 40         LDA #$40
        401B 8D 15 03      STA $0315
        401E 58            CLI
```

```
401F 60              RTS
4020 78              SEI
4021 A9 31           LDA #$31
4023 8D 14 03        STA $0314
4026 A9 EA           LDA #$EA
4028 8D 15 03        STA $0315
402B 58              CLI
402C 60              RTS
402D CE 68 40        DEC $4068
4030 F0 03           BEQ $4035
4032 4C 31 EA        JMP $EA31
4035 AD 67 40        LDA $4067
4038 8D 68 40        STA $4068
403B A2 00           LDX #$00
403D BD 00 04        LDA $0400,X
4040 18              CLC
4041 69 80           ADC #$80
4043 9D 00 04        STA $0400,X
4046 BD FF 04        LDA $04FF,X
4049 18              CLC
404A 69 80           ADC #$80
404C 9D FF 04        STA $04FF,X
404F BD FE 05        LDA $05FE,X
4052 18              CLC
4053 69 80           ADC #$80
4055 9D FE 05        STA $05FE,X
4058 BD FD 06        LDA $06FD,X
405B 18              CLC
405C 69 80           ADC #$80
405E 9D FD 06        STA $06FD,X
4061 E8              INX
4062 D0 D9           BNE $403D
4064 4C 31 EA        JMP $EA31
4067 20 D0 AD        JSR $ADD0
```
.

38. Flash colour

This routine flashes the colour of the characters between two specified colours at a specified rate.

The syntax is as follows:

    SYS 16384,colour1,colour2,rate

A rate of zero turns off the flash.

```
PAL (C)1979 BRAD TEMPLETON
2
20:     4000                         .OPT P,OO
30:     4000                         *=     $4000

                          ;
                          ;SYNTAX
                          ; SYSFLASH,COLOUR1
                          ; ,COLOUR2,NO OF
                          ; CHANGES A SECOND

80:     4000 20 FD AE             JSR   $AEFD

90:     4003 20 8A AD             JSR   $AD8A

100:    4006 20 F7 B7             JSR   $B7F7

110:    4009 A5 15                LDA   $15
110:    400B F0 03                BEQ   MORE
110:    400D 4C 48 B2             JMP   $B248

120:    4010 A5 14        MORE    LDA   $14
130:    4012 8D A5 40             STA   TEMP
140:    4015 20 FD AE             JSR   $AEFD
```

```
150:      4018 20 8A AD              JSR    $AD8A

160:      401B 20 F7 B7              JSR    $B7F7

170:      401E A5 15                 LDA    $15
180:      4020 F0 03                 BEQ    MORE1

190:      4022 4C 48 B2              JMP    $B248

200:      4025 A5 14      MORE1      LDA    $14
210:      4027 8D A6 40              STA    TEMP+
1
220:      402A 20 FD AE              JSR    $AEFD

230:      402D 20 8A AD              JSR    $AD8A

240:      4030 20 F7 B7              JSR    $B7F7

250:      4033 A5 15                 LDA    $15
260:      4035 F0 03                 BEQ    MORE2

270:      4037 4C 48 B2              JMP    $B248

280:      403A A5 14      MORE2      LDA    $14
280:      403C F0 59                 BEQ    RESET

290:      403E 8D A7 40              STA    TEMP+
2
290:      4041 78                    SEI
300:      4042 A9 54                 LDA    #<MAI
N
310:      4044 8D 14 03              STA    788
320:      4047 A9 40                 LDA    #>MAI
N
330:      4049 8D 15 03              STA    789
340:      404C 58                    CLI
350:      404D AD A7 40              LDA    TEMP+
2
350:      4050 8D A8 40              STA    TEMP+
3
360:      4053 60                    RTS
```

152

```
370:    4054              MAIN     =    *
380:    4054 CE A8 40               DEC  TEMP+
3
390:    4057 D0 29                  BNE  FINIS
H
400:    4059 AD A4 40               LDA  STORE

410:    405C CD A6 40               CMP  TEMP+
1
420:    405F F0 12                  BEQ  DO0
                             ;
440:    4061 AD A6 40               LDA  TEMP+
1
450:    4064 8D A4 40               STA  STORE

460:    4067 20 85 40               JSR  FILL
470:    406A AD A7 40               LDA  TEMP+
2
480:    406D 8D A8 40               STA  TEMP+
3
490:    4070 4C 82 40               JMP  FINIS
H
                             ;
510:    4073 AD A5 40 DO0           LDA  TEMP
520:    4076 8D A4 40               STA  STORE

530:    4079 20 85 40               JSR  FILL
540:    407C AD A7 40               LDA  TEMP+
2
550:    407F 8D A8 40               STA  TEMP+
3
                             ;
570:    4082 4C 31 EA FINISH        JMP  $EA31

                             ;
590:    4085 A2 00    FILL          LDX  #0
600:    4087 9D 00 D8 LOOP          STA  55296
,X
610:    408A 9D FF D8               STA  55296
+255,X
620:    408D 9D FE D9               STA  55296
```

```
+255+255,X
630:    4090 9D FD DA            STA  55296
+255+255+255,X
640:    4093 E8                  INX
650:    4094 D0 F1               BNE  LOOP
660:    4096 60                  RTS
                            ;
                            ;
690:    4097 78          RESET   SEI
700:    4098 A9 31               LDA  #49
710:    409A 8D 14 03            STA  788
720:    409D A9 EA               LDA  #234
730:    409F 8D 15 03            STA  789
740:    40A2 58                  CLI
750:    40A3 60                  RTS
760:    40A4 00          STORE   .BYT 0
770:    40A5             TEMP    =    *
]4000-40A5
```

READY.

```
    B*
        PC  SR AC XR YR SP
    .]97FE 72 00 00 40 F6
    .
    4000 20 FD AE      JSR $AEFD
    4003 20 8A AD      JSR $AD8A
    4006 20 F7 B7      JSR $B7F7
    4009 A5 15         LDA $15
    400B F0 03         BEQ $4010
    400D 4C 48 B2      JMP $B248
    4010 A5 14         LDA $14
    4012 8D A5 40      STA $40A5
    4015 20 FD AE      JSR $AEFD
    4018 20 8A AD      JSR $AD8A
    401B 20 F7 B7      JSR $B7F7
    401E A5 15         LDA $15
    4020 F0 03         BEQ $4025
```

```
4022 4C 48 B2       JMP $B248
4025 A5 14          LDA $14
4027 8D A6 40       STA $40A6
402A 20 FD AE       JSR $AEFD
402D 20 8A AD       JSR $AD8A
4030 20 F7 B7       JSR $B7F7
4033 A5 15          LDA $15
4035 F0 03          BEQ $403A
4037 4C 48 B2       JMP $B248
403A A5 14          LDA $14
403C F0 59          BEQ $4097
403E 8D A7 40       STA $40A7
4041 78             SEI
4042 A9 54          LDA #$54
4044 8D 14 03       STA $0314
4047 A9 40          LDA #$40
4049 8D 15 03       STA $0315
404C 58             CLI
404D AD A7 40       LDA $40A7
4050 8D A8 40       STA $40A8
4053 60             RTS
4054 CE A8 40       DEC $40A8
4057 D0 29          BNE $4082
4059 AD A4 40       LDA $40A4
405C CD A6 40       CMP $40A6
405F F0 12          BEQ $4073
4061 AD A6 40       LDA $40A6
4064 8D A4 40       STA $40A4
4067 20 85 40       JSR $4085
406A AD A7 40       LDA $40A7
406D 8D A8 40       STA $40A8
4070 4C 82 40       JMP $4082
4073 AD A5 40       LDA $40A5
4076 8D A4 40       STA $40A4
4079 20 85 40       JSR $4085
407C AD A7 40       LDA $40A7
407F 8D A8 40       STA $40A8
4082 4C 31 EA       JMP $EA31
4085 A2 00          LDX #$00
4087 9D 00 D8       STA $D800,X
408A 9D FF D8       STA $D8FF,X
```

```
408D 9D FE D9        STA $D9FE,X
4090 9D FD DA        STA $DAFD,X
4093 E8              INX
4094 D0 F1           BNE $4087
4096 60              RTS
4097 78              SEI
4098 A9 31           LDA #$31
409A 8D 14 03        STA $0314
409D A9 EA           LDA #$EA
409F 8D 15 03        STA $0315
40A2 58              CLI
40A3 60              RTS
40A4 00              BRK
```
.

39. Print at

This routine allows you to print at any position on the screen without using lots of cursor controls.

The syntax is as follows:

SYS960,X,Y,"text"

X is the column to start at and is between 0 and 39. Y is the row to start at and is between 0 and 24. The text can be text in quotes, strings, numbers, variables or any other legal print statement.

```
PAL (C)1979 BRAD TEMPLETON
2
20:      03C0                        .OPT P,00
30:      03C0                        *=   960
                          ;
                          ;PRINT AT ROUTINE
60:      03C0 20 FD AE          JSR  $AEFD
70:      03C3 20 9E B7          JSR  $B79E
80:      03C6 8A               TXA
90:      03C7 48               PHA
100:     03C8 20 FD AE          JSR  $AEFD
110:     03CB 20 9E B7          JSR  $B79E
120:     03CE 8A               TXA
130:     03CF A8               TAY
140:     03D0 68               PLA
150:     03D1 AA               TAX
160:     03D2 18               CLC
170:     03D3 20 F0 FF          JSR  $FFF0
180:     03D6 20 FD AE          JSR  $AEFD
190:     03D9 4C A0 AA          JMP  $AAA0
```

```
200:    03DC 00                      BRK
]03C0-03DD

READY.



          B*
             PC   SR AC XR YR SP
          .]97FE 72 00 00 40 F6
          .
          03C0 20 FD AE       JSR $AEFD
          03C3 20 9E B7       JSR $B79E
          03C6 8A             TXA
          03C7 48             PHA
          03C8 20 FD AE       JSR $AEFD
          03CB 20 9E B7       JSR $B79E
          03CE 8A             TXA
          03CF A8             TAY
          03D0 68             PLA
          03D1 AA             TAX
          03D2 18             CLC
          03D3 20 F0 FF       JSR $FFF0
          03D6 20 FD AE       JSR $AEFD
          03D9 4C A0 AA       JMP $AAA0
          03DC 00             BRK
          .
```

40. Split screen

This routine sets up a raster scan that allows the text and high res screen to coexist at the same time. You can specify where the cut is to take place and whether text or high res is at the top.

The syntax is as follows:

SYS 16384, line for change,option

where line is the line down the screen (the same as the Y coordinates for plot) and option is 1 for the text to be at the top and 0 for the text to be at the bottom. If line has the value 0 then the raster is switched off. The line number must be in the range 50 to 249.

```
PAL (C)1979 BRAD TEMPLETON
2
20:     4000                            .OPT P,00
30:     4000                            *=   *4000
                                  ;
                                  ;RASTER TO ALLOW SPLIT
                                  ;SCREENS
                                  ;SYNTAX
                                  ;
                                  ;SYS16384,CHANGE,1=
                                  ;TEXT/0=HIRES
110:    4000 20 FD AE              JSR  *AEFD
120:    4003 20 8A AD              JSR  *AD8A
130:    4006 20 F7 B7              JSR  *B7F7
                                  ;
150:    4009 A5 15                LDA  *15
160:    400B D0 2B                BNE  IQERR
170:    400D A5 14                LDA  *14
180:    400F D0 03                BNE  MOR
180:    4011 4C A5 40             JMP  RESET
```

```
190:   4014 C9 31      MOR       CMP   #49
200:   4016 90 20                BCC   IQERR
210:   4018 C9 FA                CMP   #250
220:   401A B0 1C                BCS   IQERR
230:   401C 8D FE 40             STA   TEMP

250:   401F 20 FD AE             JSR   $AEFD
260:   4022 20 8A AD             JSR   $AD8A
270:   4025 20 F7 B7             JSR   $B7F7
280:   4028 A5 15                LDA   $15
290:   402A D0 0C                BNE   IQERR
300:   402C A5 14                LDA   $14
310:   402E C9 02                CMP   #2
320:   4030 B0 06                BCS   IQERR
330:   4032 8D FF 40             STA   TEMP+1
340:   4035 4C 3B 40             JMP   MORE
350:   4038 4C 48 B2   IQERR     JMP   $B248
360:   403B AD FE 40   MORE      LDA   TEMP
370:   403E 8D F8 40             STA   RASTER
380:   4041 AD FF 40             LDA   TEMP+1
390:   4044 C9 01                CMP   #1
400:   4046 F0 17                BEQ   TEXTTOP
410:   4048 A9 08                LDA   #8
410:   404A A2 15                LDX   #21
420:   404C 8D FA 40             STA   TEXT
420:   404F 8E FB 40             STX   TEXT+1
430:   4052 A9 3B                LDA   #59
430:   4054 A2 1B                LDX   #27
440:   4056 8D FC 40             STA   HIRES
440:   4059 8E FD 40             STX   HIRES+1
450:   405C 4C 73 40             JMP   SETUP
460:   405F A9 15     TEXTTOP    LDA   #21
460:   4061 A2 08                LDX   #8
470:   4063 8D FA 40             STA   TEXT
470:   4066 8E FB 40             STX   TEXT+1
480:   4069 A9 1B                LDA   #27
480:   406B A2 3B                LDX   #59
490:   406D 8D FC 40             STA   HIRES
490:   4070 8E FD 40             STX   HIRES+1
                                 ;
510:   4073            SETUP     =     *
```

```
520:    4073 78                         SEI
530:    4074 A9 7F                      LDA   #$7F
540:    4076 8D 0D DC                   STA   $DC0D
550:    4079 A9 01                      LDA   #$01
560:    407B 8D 1A D0                   STA   $D01A
570:    407E A9 02                      LDA   #$02
580:    4080 85 FB                      STA   $FB
590:    4082 AD F8 40                   LDA   RASTER
600:    4085 8D 12 D0                   STA   $D012
610:    4088 A9 18                      LDA   #$18
620:    408A 8D 11 D0                   STA   $D011
630:    408D AD 14 03                   LDA   $0314
640:    4090 8D F6 40                   STA   FIN-2
650:    4093 AD 15 03                   LDA   $0315
660:    4096 8D F7 40                   STA   FIN-1
670:    4099 A9 C6                      LDA   #<MAIN
680:    409B 8D 14 03                   STA   788
690:    409E A9 40                      LDA   #>MAIN
700:    40A0 8D 15 03                   STA   789
710:    40A3 58                         CLI
720:    40A4 60                         RTS
730:    40A5 78           RESET         SEI
730:    40A6 A9 31                      LDA   #49
740:    40A8 8D 14 03                   STA   788
750:    40AB A9 EA                      LDA   #234
750:    40AD 8D 15 03                   STA   789
760:    40B0 A9 15                      LDA   #21
760:    40B2 8D 18 D0                   STA   53272
770:    40B5 A9 1B                      LDA   #27
770:    40B7 8D 11 D0                   STA   53265
780:    40BA A9 00                      LDA   #0
780:    40BC 8D 1A D0                   STA   $D01A
790:    40BF A9 80                      LDA   #128
790:    40C1 8D 0D DC                   STA   56333
800:    40C4 58                         CLI
800:    40C5 60                         RTS
810:    40C6 AD 19 D0     MAIN          LDA   $D019
820:    40C9 8D 19 D0                   STA   $D019
830:    40CC 29 01                      AND   #$01
840:    40CE F0 1F                      BEQ   LOOP
850:    40D0 C6 FB                      DEC   $FB
```

161

```
860:    40D2 10 04          BPL    LOOP9
870:    40D4 A9 01          LDA    #$01
880:    40D6 85 FB          STA    $FB
890:    40D8 A6 FB    LOOP9 LDX    $FB
900:    40DA BD F8 40       LDA    RASTER,X
910:    40DD 8D 12 D0       STA    $D012
920:    40E0 BD FA 40       LDA    TEXT,X
930:    40E3 8D 18 D0       STA    53272
940:    40E6 BD FC 40       LDA    HIRES,X
950:    40E9 8D 11 D0       STA    $D011
960:    40EC 8A             TXA
970:    40ED F0 06          BEQ    LOOP1
980:    40EF 68      LOOP   PLA
990:    40F0 A8             TAY
1000:   40F1 68             PLA
1010:   40F2 AA             TAX
1020:   40F3 68             PLA
1030:   40F4 40             RTI
1040:   40F5 4C 31 EA LOOP1 JMP    $EA31
1040:   40F8          FIN    =      *
1050:   40F8 96 00    RASTER .BYT   150,0
1060:   40FA 08 15    TEXT   .BYT   8,21
1070:   40FC 3B 1B    HIRES  .BYT   59,27
1080:   40FE 00 00    TEMP   .WORD0
]4000-4100
```

READY.

```
        .
4000 20 FD AE       JSR   $AEFD
4003 20 8A AD       JSR   $AD8A
4006 20 F7 B7       JSR   $B7F7
4009 A5 15          LDA   $15
400B D0 2B          BNE   $4038
400D A5 14          LDA   $14
400F D0 03          BNE   $4014
4011 4C A5 40       JMP   $40A5
4014 C9 31          CMP   #$31
```

```
4016 90 20        BCC  $4038
4018 C9 FA        CMP  #$FA
401A B0 1C        BCS  $4038
401C 8D FE 40     STA  $40FE
401F 20 FD AE     JSR  $AEFD
4022 20 8A AD     JSR  $AD8A
4025 20 F7 B7     JSR  $B7F7
4028 A5 15        LDA  $15
402A D0 0C        BNE  $4038
402C A5 14        LDA  $14
402E C9 02        CMP  #$02
4030 B0 06        BCS  $4038
4032 8D FF 40     STA  $40FF
4035 4C 3B 40     JMP  $403B
4038 4C 48 B2     JMP  $B248
403B AD FE 40     LDA  $40FE
403E 8D F8 40     STA  $40F8
4041 AD FF 40     LDA  $40FF
4044 C9 01        CMP  #$01
4046 F0 17        BEQ  $405F
4048 A9 08        LDA  #$08
404A A2 15        LDX  #$15
404C 8D FA 40     STA  $40FA
404F 8E FB 40     STX  $40FB
4052 A9 3B        LDA  #$3B
4054 A2 1B        LDX  #$1B
4056 8D FC 40     STA  $40FC
4059 8E FD 40     STX  $40FD
405C 4C 73 40     JMP  $4073
405F A9 15        LDA  #$15
4061 A2 08        LDX  #$08
4063 8D FA 40     STA  $40FA
4066 8E FB 40     STX  $40FB
4069 A9 1B        LDA  #$1B
406B A2 3B        LDX  #$3B
406D 8D FC 40     STA  $40FC
4070 8E FD 40     STX  $40FD
4073 78           SEI
4074 A9 7F        LDA  #$7F
4076 8D 0D DC     STA  $DC0D
4079 A9 01        LDA  #$01
```

```
407B 8D 1A DØ      STA $DØ1A
407E A9 Ø2         LDA #$Ø2
4080 85 FB         STA $FB
4082 AD F8 40      LDA $40F8
4085 8D 12 DØ      STA $DØ12
4088 A9 18         LDA #$18
408A 8D 11 DØ      STA $DØ11
408D AD 14 Ø3      LDA $Ø314
4090 8D F6 40      STA $40F6
4093 AD 15 Ø3      LDA $Ø315
4096 8D F7 40      STA $40F7
4099 A9 C6         LDA #$C6
409B 8D 14 Ø3      STA $Ø314
409E A9 40         LDA #$40
40AØ 8D 15 Ø3      STA $Ø315
40A3 58            CLI
40A4 60            RTS
40A5 78            SEI
40A6 A9 31         LDA #$31
40A8 8D 14 Ø3      STA $Ø314
40AB A9 EA         LDA #$EA
40AD 8D 15 Ø3      STA $Ø315
40BØ A9 15         LDA #$15
40B2 8D 18 DØ      STA $DØ18
40B5 A9 1B         LDA #$1B
40B7 8D 11 DØ      STA $DØ11
40BA A9 ØØ         LDA #$ØØ
40BC 8D 1A DØ      STA $DØ1A
40BF A9 80         LDA #$80
40C1 8D ØD DC      STA $DCØD
40C4 58            CLI
40C5 60            RTS
40C6 AD 19 DØ      LDA $DØ19
40C9 8D 19 DØ      STA $DØ19
40CC 29 Ø1         AND #$Ø1
40CE FØ 1F         BEQ $40EF
40DØ C6 FB         DEC $FB
40D2 1Ø Ø4         BPL $40D8
40D4 A9 Ø1         LDA #$Ø1
40D6 85 FB         STA $FB
40D8 A6 FB         LDX $FB
```

164

```
40DA BD F8 40      LDA $40F8,X
40DD 8D 12 D0      STA $D012
40E0 BD FA 40      LDA $40FA,X
40E3 8D 18 D0      STA $D018
40E6 BD FC 40      LDA $40FC,X
40E9 8D 11 D0      STA $D011
40EC 8A            TXA
40ED F0 06         BEQ $40F5
40EF 68            PLA
40F0 A8            TAY
40F1 68            PLA
40F2 AA            TAX
40F3 68            PLA
40F4 40            RTI
40F5 4C 31 EA      JMP $EA31
  .
  .
  .:40F8 96 00 08 15 3B 1B 00 00
  .
```

You may also enjoy...

Mastering the Commodore 64

Mark Greenshields

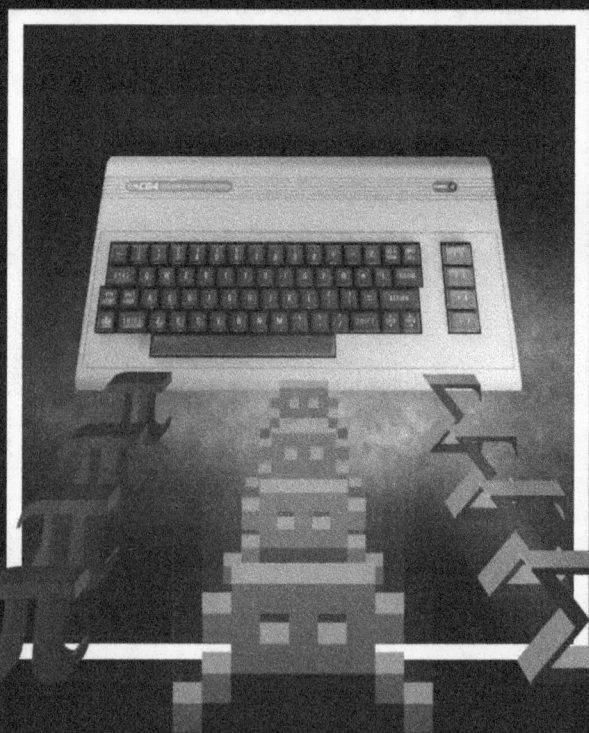

www.ingramcontent.com/pod-product-compliance
Lightning Source LLC
Chambersburg PA
CBHW030014290326
41934CB00005B/337